# The Atlas of
# War and Peace

Dan Smith

with
Ane Bræin

Earthscan Publications Ltd, London

This fourth edition first published in the UK in 2003
by Earthscan Publications Ltd

A catalogue record for this book is available from the British Library
ISBN: 1 84407 000 X

Produced for Earthscan Publications Ltd by Myriad Editions Limited
6–7 Old Steine, Brighton BN1 1EJ, UK
http://www.MyriadEditions.com

Edited and coordinated for Myriad Editions by
Paul Jeremy and Candida Lacey
Design and graphics by Paul Jeremy, Isabelle Lewis and Corinne Pearlman
Cartography by Isabelle Lewis

Printed and bound in Hong Kong
under the supervision of Bob Cassels, The Hanway Press, London

For a full list of publications please contact:

Earthscan Publications Ltd
120 Pentonville Road, London, N1 9JN, UK
tel:  +44 (0)20 7278 0433
fax: +44 (0)20 7278 1142
email:  earthinfo@earthscan.co.uk
http://www.earthscan.co.uk

Earthscan is an editorially independent subsidiary of Kogan Page Ltd and publishes in association
with WWF-UK and the International Institute for Environment and Development

# CONTENTS

# INTRODUCTION

At rare moments it seems a new era is starting before our eyes and history is about to change very fast. September 11, 2001, was such a moment, when the twin towers of the World Trade Center in New York and a part of the Pentagon in Washington, D.C., were destroyed, killing over 3,000 people. The attacks were brutal and ruthless, and the attackers did not care that among the many nationalities killed were their compatriots and co-religionists.

For people who try to understand what goes on in the world, two obstacles to understanding 9/11 were immediately evident. One was that the grief, the pain, and the horror of that moment may have clouded many people's eyes. The other was that the event was so large that many people may have disconnected what came after it from what went before, as if 9/11 created a completely new world.

The grief and the emotion not only made it hard for many, and especially hard for many Americans, to understand why this had happened. Watching and reading the first media coverage of September 11, 2001, it seemed there was great difficulty in even asking why it happened. For to ask why presupposes that there is an answer, and that this answer would propose a reason, which would imply the attacks were a rational act – and how could such horror be rational?

But war is full of both horror and of rational calculation; thousands are killed and for a reason. Many acts of violence are blind and unreasoning, but many are open-eyed and the result of hard thought – and perhaps all the more cruel for that.

To say such actions are – or may be – the result of calculation does not, of course, make them right, and does not even mean they are intelligent. Those who use violence are often not only blinded to the moral dimension, sometimes because moral faculties have been dulled by acts of violence committed against them, they are also blind to the consequences of their actions. Time and again we see a carefully calculated and planned act of violence – used to achieve a specific effect – have a very different result from the one intended. Attacks that are meant to suppress terrorism simply encourage it. Attacks that are meant to dissuade people from supporting an uprising simply help the insurgents find more recruits. Attacks meant to create security destroy it.

So the attacks on 9/11 were calculated actions, which means they had a purpose, but does not necessarily mean they have achieved it. The purpose of the attacks is visible from the targets – the financial and the strategic power of the USA – and, it has been inferred from the available evidence and from the statements of Osama bin Laden, leader of the al Qaida network, that the fourth hijacked aircraft on September 11, 2001 was to be aimed at a political target. The aim, it seems, was to deliver a blow to the USA

that would start the process of forcing it out of the Middle East, and specifically out of Saudi Arabia, and at the same time sound the clarion call for Islamic unity against the USA.

What the attacks initially achieved beyond the suffering they caused, and after the first shock had dissipated, was to unite most of the world against al Qaida and in support of a US-led offensive on the network's bases and backers in Afghanistan. That offensive was partly successful – bin Laden was not captured but the Taliban regime that gave him sanctuary was thrown out of power.

If there is in all this some kind of success for al Qaida, it is a paradoxical one. The USA did not respond to 9/11 by pulling back but by advancing further, not only going into Afghanistan, but also expanding its military presence in several parts of the world, not least in the Middle East and Central Asia. These widely spread forces not only demonstrate the extraordinary and unique power of US armed forces but also make the American target bigger for those who are determined, ruthless, and clever enough to find a way to attack it. Yet those attacks, when they come, will likely only cause the USA to project its power yet more widely and yet more forcefully.

The historical dimensions of an event as enormous as 9/11 are hard to gauge quickly and are usually overstated in the immediate aftermath. Nonetheless, it is clear that 9/11 marked the end of an interval between two eras, an interval that began just twelve years before. In November 1989, the Berlin Wall was breached and the Cold War came to an end. The long decade of the 1990s began with bits of debris being taken home not only as souvenirs of an historical moment but also as tokens of the possibility of peace and of liberty. Ground Zero in Manhattan and the collapse of the World Trade Center's two towers mark the end of that long decade.

We do not yet have a name for the new era but that it has begun is undoubted. However, as we acknowledge the historical shift with the end of the long decade of the 1990s, we also need to acknowledge that much remains the same. Many of the wars active at the start of the twenty-first century were more than a decade old, with causes lying still further back. Many of them derive from failures in the economic and political systems where they occur. Some of the explanations of those economic and political failures lie in the way the world is weighted against those with less wealth. Some of the explanations lie in weaknesses within the societies themselves, weaknesses that were not created by global injustices, even though those injustices may make the weaknesses worse.

When the Cold War ended in 1989, it became more possible to see these conflicts in their own light – and their own right, as political problems that were not significant according to what part they played in superpower rivalry, but because they are human tragedies and humanitarian disasters. And with the end of the Cold War it became more possible to take action to try to end these wars and to develop the possibility for a decent way of life for the ordinary people of countries long torn apart by war.

Alongside these old wars of the Cold War era, that actually had very little to do with the Cold War, the long decade of the 1990s was marked by new wars that came as the Cold War ended. The breakup of the USSR and of the old Yugoslavia generated vicious wars throughout the 1990s. Some of them persisted after 9/11, others have been suppressed, but the problems that caused them are only being controlled, not solved. Even an event as cataclysmic as 9/11 does not change everything: as well as the new monsters of the new era, the old monsters linger on from before the end of the Cold War and from the inter-era interval of the 1990s.

The previous era, before the Wall came down, was characterized by a bi-polar conflict between two contenders for world power – the USA and the USSR. The new era is characterized by the USA's overwhelming military predominance. No other state is anywhere near as powerful in military terms as the USA, but as all now know, for it is one of the lessons of 9/11, unparalleled power does not make the USA invulnerable. Power and security are two different things.

That is perhaps the simple thought that lies at the heart of this atlas. Power can be used for good or for ill, and the country with by far the most power in the world is the USA. The standard by which its use of that power must be judged is security in its most basic and ordinary sense – the security of ordinary people to live decent lives.

This atlas is the fourth edition in a line that began in 1983. Then, depicting a world of war and peace was largely a matter of taking a global view of the bi-polar rivalry and seeing who took what side with what forces. As the world has changed over two decades, I have found that trying to depict a world of war and peace means focusing a little less on the global and the general, and a little more on the regional and the particular. This makes things look more complicated. After twenty years of working on these atlases, I confess I am not sure whether things just look more complicated, or whether they actually are more complicated.

The opening three chapters take a general view. The first chapter looks at some global trends in the causes of armed conflict, while the next looks into the world of military hardware and power, and the third outlines some of the human and moral issues. The next five chapters take a region each and consider the dynamics of war-making and of peace-making. The last chapter returns to the global view, and takes a more general look at how peace is built. I hope the atlas manages to strike a balance between the general and the particular – and especially that its tenable generalizations will not offend too many specialists. Out of it I hope only that a few fundamental thoughts emerge: about the conditions that create violent conflict; about the political leadership that is needed to build peaceful relations; and about the myths and dangers of pursuing security purely through violence and the projection of power, whether in a small region of an impoverished country or on a global scale.

I have received a great deal of help in preparing this fourth edition. Colleagues at the International Peace Research Institute, Oslo (PRIO) have offered me useful advice and sources of information – here I especially want to thank Pavel Baev, Scott Gates, Nils Petter Gleditsch, Kristian Berg Harpviken, Wenche Hauge, Nic Marsh, Ananda Millard, Håvard Strand, and Stein Tønnesson, the Institute's director. Jill Lewis showed me where the data on HIV/AIDS and conflict were to be found. Berit Tolleshaug kept the data on armed conflicts up to date, following earlier work by Kristin Ingstad Sandberg, Cecilie Sundby and Olav Høgberg, and Karen Hostens. My boundless gratitude goes to all of them, with the necessary rider that they are only responsible for the things that I got right, while any errors are all my own.

Ane Bræin started out working on the atlas as my research assistant, but quickly began to make a substantive input into decisions about data and presentation. She shares in the credit for this atlas on the title page because the work she ended up doing is more than is in an assistant's job description. I want to thank her for that effort and commitment, and also for being a pleasure to work with. It is not enjoyable to trawl through the evidence of people's capacity to inflict pain and suffering, and it is good to have a working companion along the way.

Myriad Editions looked after the process of taking words and figures and transforming them into maps. The creative team at Myriad is highly professional and quite astonishingly good humored about my habit of pushing every deadline to the wall, through it, and out the other side. As Creative Director Corinne Pearlman infuses Myriad's work with style and incisiveness; Isabelle Lewis has provided inspired cartographic design; Paul Jeremy is an editor who knows how to interpret the raw material in such a way as to find its best possibilities; and Candida Lacey runs the company with verve and efficiency and a human touch through which I have found a good friend. I thank them all for the pleasure of working with them.

Dan Smith
Oslo
November 2002

# CHAPTER ONE

# The Causes of War

A NEW HISTORICAL ERA began as the Cold War ended in 1989. Initial hopes in the West that this would be a new era of peace fell as awareness grew of vicious wars in the Third World, in the former Soviet Union and in southeastern Europe. Since the end of the Cold War, there have been more than 120 wars worldwide.

In part, there was more awareness of these wars than there had been in the past simply because there were more of them. In the early 1990s, the annual number of armed conflicts increased sharply compared to a few years previously. By mid-decade, however, the pace was slowing and the annual total began to decline. By the turn of the millennium, the world was experiencing about as many wars as there had been just before the Cold War ended.

In part, there was more awareness of these wars because, with the Cold War out of the way, people could see what was going on. For most of the second half of the 20th century, the great confrontation between the USA and the USSR and their respective alliance systems had led many people to interpret the world in the light of the East-West conflict. Whatever did not fit into that framework was all too likely to be ignored.

Fewer than ten percent of contemporary wars are between states. Wars of independence from colonial power are almost completely a thing of the past, though there are many wars of secession, in which the leaders of one region or ethnic group in a state try to break away from it. International war inevitably

**Armed conflicts 1990–2001**

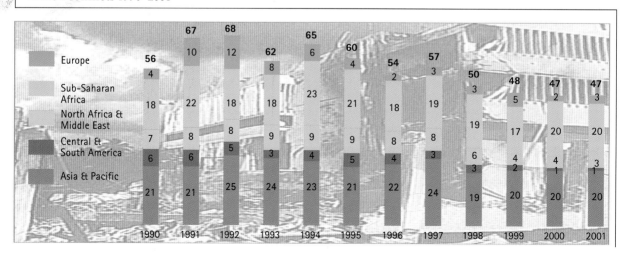

| | Europe | Sub-Saharan Africa | North Africa & Middle East | Central & South America | Asia & Pacific |
|---|---|---|---|---|---|
| 1990 (56) | 4 | 18 | 7 | 6 | 21 |
| 1991 (67) | 10 | 22 | 8 | 6 | 21 |
| 1992 (68) | 12 | 18 | 8 | 5 | 25 |
| 1993 (62) | 8 | 18 | 9 | 3 | 24 |
| 1994 (65) | 6 | 23 | 9 | 4 | 23 |
| 1995 (60) | 4 | 21 | 9 | 5 | 21 |
| 1996 (54) | 2 | 18 | 8 | 4 | 22 |
| 1997 (57) | 3 | 19 | 8 | 3 | 24 |
| 1998 (50) | 3 | 19 | 6 | 3 | 19 |
| 1999 (48) | 5 | 17 | 4 | 2 | 20 |
| 2000 (47) | 2 | 20 | 4 | 1 | 20 |
| 2001 (47) | 3 | 20 | 3 | 1 | 20 |

gets enormous media coverage, not only because of its evident importance, but also because of its rarity value, but almost all wars today are fought within states rather than between them.

People do not take up arms easily. The decision to go to war is generally complex and involves many different factors. Only two things are necessary for war to occur – a disagreement, and the means with which to fight over it. On the other hand, the nature of the disagreement and the factors that tip it over into violence are extremely varied.

It is this wide variety of possible causes that makes war hard to understand. It is the reason why even some wars in recent years that have been confidently predicted by every expert seem to take international political leaders by surprise.

When trying to understand wars, it helps to divide up the causes into different types. There are the background causes, the issues that build up over decades, the problems that build a powder keg just waiting to be ignited. Then there are the political factors, the behaviour of political leaders and movements, their goals and the way they pursue them. These make the fuse to the explosive, just waiting for the spark. And then there are the triggers, unpredictable by their nature – possibly a deliberate act intended to start a war, but more often a virtual accident, such as an assassination, or a demonstration that becomes a riot, or a police action that becomes a massacre, or even a change in the world price of an important commodity. They are the match that lights the fuse.

The following four maps look at background causes. Political behaviour and the triggers of open war are covered in Chapters 4 to 8.

The first maps help us find the long-term, background causes of war in the combination of poor economic conditions and a lack of political openings through which to seek change peacefully. What we see here is a foundation of injustice. The more that a country's resources are stretched, the sharper is the competition for them, and the weaker is the state's ability to meet most people's needs. This gives rise to grievance, to a sense of injustice and frustration. It is fertile soil for ambitious political leaders, articulating grievance, voicing a sense of injustice, whether or not they share in the feelings of their followers.

People commit themselves to these leaders because they believe that doing so offers a chance to redress the injustice they see in their own lives. If they are lucky, their leaders will manage to avoid committing them to a war. Too often, especially in poor countries, and where democracy is uncertain, the people are unlucky in their leaders. In a more just world, where the divisions between the rich and poor were not so great, they would not have to trust to luck.

# I | Poverty

Wars today are concentrated in the poorest countries.

• Of those countries classified by the United Nations Human Development Report as showing high development in 2000, two percent experienced civil war in 1997-2001.

• Of those countries with medium development, 30 percent experienced civil war in 1997-2001.

• Of those with low development, 56 percent experienced civil war in 1997-2001.

There is more war in poor countries partly because people cannot meet their needs as easily as in richer countries. Competition for resources is fiercer and more desperate. Poorer countries have less opportunity than richer countries to develop political institutions to absorb conflict and channel it in non-violent directions. And in the poorest regions, young men may find that joining the rebels gives them security and even privileges that are not available to them if they live a normal life.

Insurgent forces that claim to speak for the poor often exploit them brutally. Those who are richer and more powerful than others can go to great lengths to protect what they have and grab some more. And poor countries are less able than rich ones to protect themselves against being looted by ruthless individuals.

RUSSIA

UKRAINE

MOLDOVA

GEORGIA

AZERBAIJAN

KAZAKHSTAN

MONGOLIA

JAPAN

SOUTH
KOREA

see inset

ARMENIA

IRAN

UZBEKISTAN

TURKMENISTAN

KYRGYZSTAN

TAJIKISTAN

CHINA

AFGHANISTAN

PAKISTAN

BAHRAIN

QATAR

UAE

SAUDI
ARABIA

OMAN

NEPAL

BHUTAN

INDIA

BANGLADESH

BURMA

Hong Kong

SUDAN

ERITREA

YEMEN

DJIBOUTI

SOMALIA

LAOS

VIETNAM

THAILAND

CAMBODIA

PHILIPPINES

DEMOCRATIC
REPUBLIC OF
CONGO

UGANDA

KENYA

MALDIVES

SRI LANKA

SAMOA

FIJI

RWANDA

TANZANIA

COMOROS

BRUNEI

MALAYSIA

SINGAPORE

INDONESIA

PAPUA
NEW
GUINEA

BURUNDI

ZAMBIA

MALAWI

MADAGASCAR

MAURITIUS

EAST TIMOR

ZIMBABWE

BOTSWANA

MOZAMBIQUE

SWAZILAND

SOUTH
AFRICA

LESOTHO

AUSTRALIA

NEW ZEALAND

TURKEY

CYPRUS

LEBANON

SYRIA

ISRAEL

JORDAN

IRAQ

KUWAIT

EGYPT

SAUDI
ARABIA

11

# 2 | Rights

CANADA

USA

Arbitrary arrest
and detention after
11 September 2001.

MEXICO

BAHAMAS

CUBA

JAMAICA

BELIZE
HONDURAS
GUATEMALA

EL SALVADOR    NICARAGUA

HAITI

DOMINICAN
REPUBLIC

ST LUCIA

TRINIDAD & TOBAGO

VENEZUELA

GUYANA
SURINAME

COLOMBIA

ECUADOR

PERU

BRAZIL

BOLIVIA

CHILE    PARAGUAY

ARGENTINA    URUGUAY

IRELAND    UNITED
KINGDOM

SWE

GERMANY

BELGIUM

FRANCE  SWITZ.  AUST
SLOVENIA

ITALY

SPAIN

PORTUGAL

MAL

TUNISIA

MOROCCO

ALGERIA    LIBY

MAURITANIA

NIGER

SENEGAL

GAMBIA

GUINEA-
BISSAU    GUINEA

BURKINA
FASO

SIERRA LEONE

LIBERIA

CÔTE d'
IVOIRE

GHANA

TOGO
BENIN

NIGERIA

CAMEROON

EQUATORIAL
GUINEA

CONGO

ANGO

NAMI

War and the extreme abuse of
human rights abuse go hand
in hand. At the turn of the millennium:

• There were reports of extra-judicial
executions by 72 percent of states involved
in civil wars.

• Of states accused of grave abuses of
human rights in the form of arbitrary arrest,
police and prison violence, and mistreatment
of refugees and immigrants, six percent
experienced civil war.

• Of states accused of torture, 30 percent
experienced civil war.

• Of states accused of extra-judicial
executions (of political opponents, prisoners

of war and the socially undesirable),
58 percent experienced civil war.

When a state uses extreme violence,
opposition to the ruling system first takes
the form of silence. If the conditions that
created dissatisfaction get worse, even the
most extreme official violence may not
suppress all opposition and then the
opposition has no option but violence.

When war has started, the first instinct of
most governments is to clamp down on
freedoms – of information, of debate, of
protest. In some cases, the clampdown
becomes extreme.

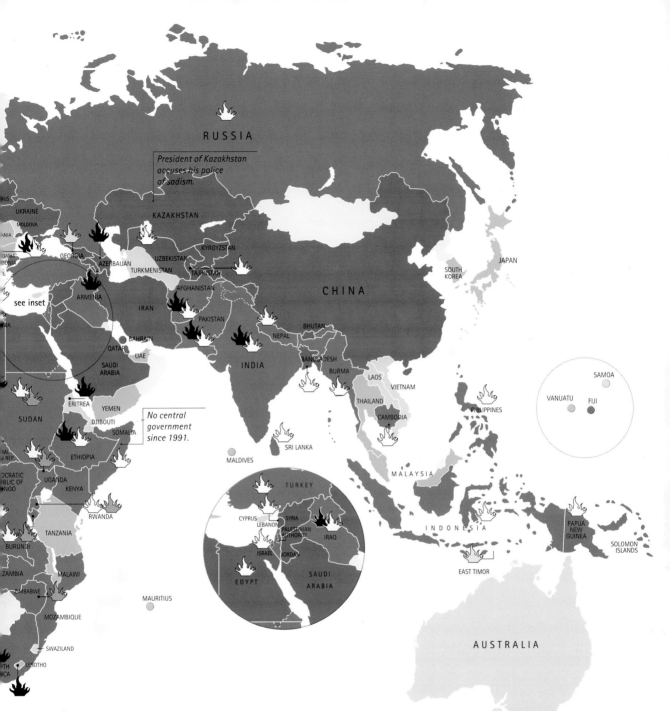

President of Kazakhstan accuses his police of sadism.

No central government since 1991.

see inset

## Extreme abuse of human rights 1998-2000

States whose reported abuses of human rights include

- extra-judicial executions
- torture
- arbitrary arrest and detention
- mistreatment by police and/or prison authorities
- violent and/or abusive treatment of refugees, asylum seekers and/or immigrants

no data or no human rights abuse

## Wars 1997–2001

Between 1997 and 2001 the country was involved in

 war with another state

 civil war

 intervention in another country's civil war

 a war of independence

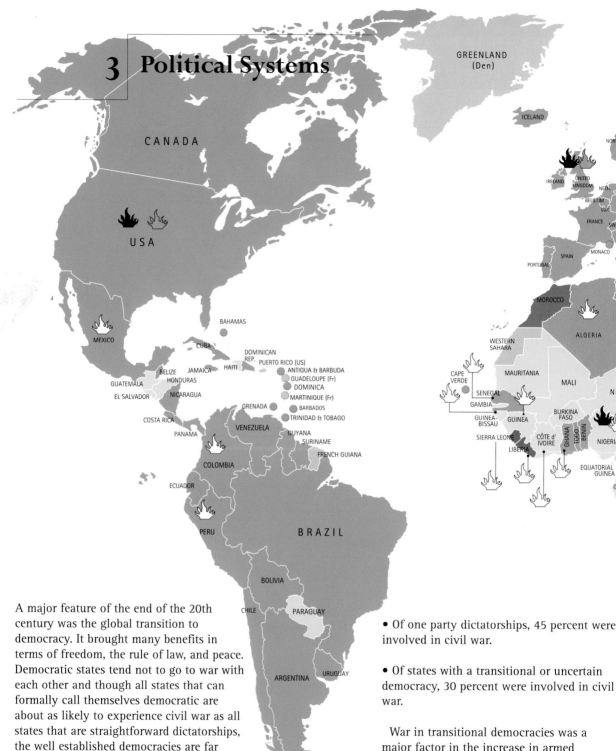

GREENLAND
(Den)

ICELAND

NORWAY

IRELAND   UNITED
          KINGDOM   DENMARK

          NETH.        GERMAN

          BELGIUM
          LUX.

FRANCE   SWITZ.   SLOVEN
                  CRO
                  ITA

PORTUGAL   SPAIN   MONACO

                          TUNISIA

MOROCCO

WESTERN        ALGERIA      LIB
SAHARA

CAPE        MAURITANIA    MALI
VERDE
      SENEGAL                NIGER
      GAMBIA
GUINEA-          BURKINA
BISSAU   GUINEA  FASO
                 GHANA  BENIN
SIERRA LEONE  CÔTE d'  TOGO  NIGERIA
LIBERIA       IVOIRE
                      EQUATORIAL  CAMEROO
                      GUINEA
                              GABON
                              CONG

                              ANG

                          NAMI

CANADA

USA

BAHAMAS

MEXICO       CUBA
                   DOMINICAN
                   REP.  PUERTO RICO (US)
BELIZE   JAMAICA  HAITI   ANTIGUA & BARBUDA
GUATEMALA HONDURAS        GUADELOUPE (Fr)
                          DOMINICA
EL SALVADOR  NICARAGUA    MARTINIQUE (Fr)
          GRENADA         BARBADOS
COSTA RICA                TRINIDAD & TOBAGO
PANAMA   VENEZUELA  GUYANA
                    SURINAME
          COLOMBIA       FRENCH GUIANA

ECUADOR

PERU          BRAZIL

          BOLIVIA

CHILE    PARAGUAY

          ARGENTINA  URUGUAY

FALKLAND
ISLANDS (UK)

A major feature of the end of the 20th century was the global transition to democracy. It brought many benefits in terms of freedom, the rule of law, and peace. Democratic states tend not to go to war with each other and though all states that can formally call themselves democratic are about as likely to experience civil war as all states that are straightforward dictatorships, the well established democracies are far more stable than dictatorships. However, while democracy is relatively safe from war, the path to it is full of dangers. At the turn of the millennium:

• Of established democracies, 12 percent were involved in civil war.

• Of one party dictatorships, 45 percent were involved in civil war.

• Of states with a transitional or uncertain democracy, 30 percent were involved in civil war.

War in transitional democracies was a major factor in the increase in armed conflict during the 1990s, especially in the former USSR and ex-Yugoslavia. When the rules of the game are not clear, not accepted by all parties, and not well established, political rivalries are pursued by any means possible. Electoral defeat – or its expectation – may be the spur to war.

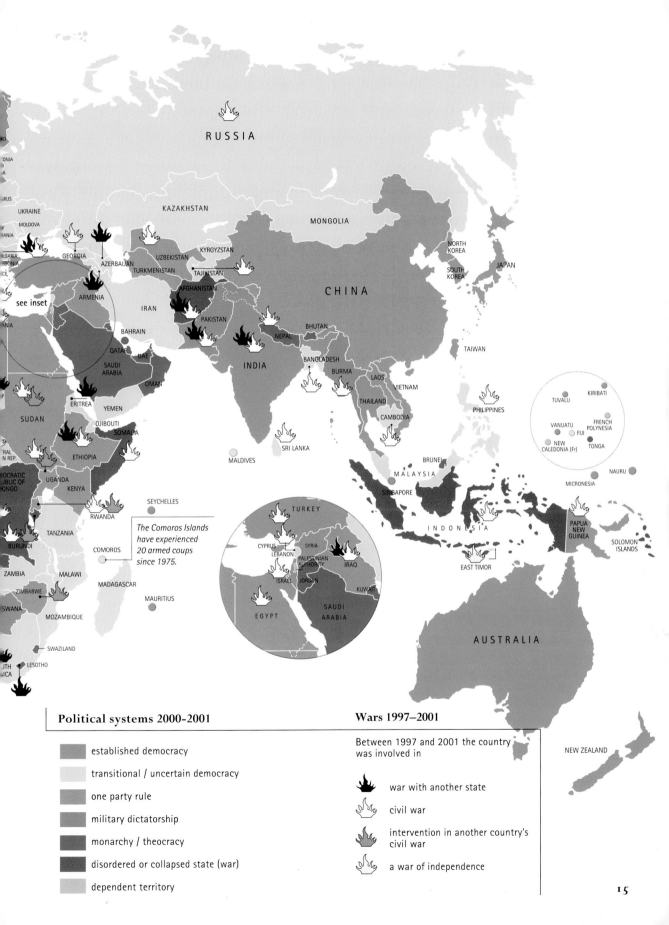

RUSSIA

UKRAINE

MOLDOVA

KAZAKHSTAN

MONGOLIA

NORTH KOREA

SOUTH KOREA

JAPAN

GEORGIA

AZERBAIJAN

UZBEKISTAN

KYRGYZSTAN

TURKMENISTAN

TAJIKISTAN

CHINA

ARMENIA

IRAN

AFGHANISTAN

PAKISTAN

NEPAL

BHUTAN

TAIWAN

see inset

BAHRAIN

QATAR

UAE

SAUDI ARABIA

OMAN

INDIA

BANGLADESH

BURMA

LAOS

VIETNAM

ERITREA

YEMEN

DJIBOUTI

SOMALIA

SUDAN

ETHIOPIA

UGANDA

KENYA

THAILAND

CAMBODIA

PHILIPPINES

TUVALU

KIRIBATI

VANUATU

FRENCH POLYNESIA

FIJI

NEW CALEDONIA (Fr)

TONGA

NAURU

MICRONESIA

SRI LANKA

MALDIVES

BRUNEI

MALAYSIA

SINGAPORE

SEYCHELLES

RWANDA

The Comoros Islands have experienced 20 armed coups since 1975.

COMOROS

TANZANIA

BURUNDI

ZAMBIA

MALAWI

ZIMBABWE

MADAGASCAR

MAURITIUS

MOZAMBIQUE

SWAZILAND

LESOTHO

INDONESIA

EAST TIMOR

PAPUA NEW GUINEA

SOLOMON ISLANDS

AUSTRALIA

NEW ZEALAND

**Inset:**

TURKEY

CYPRUS

LEBANON

SYRIA

PALESTINIAN AUTHORITY

IRAQ

ISRAEL

JORDAN

KUWAIT

EGYPT

SAUDI ARABIA

## Political systems 2000-2001

- established democracy
- transitional / uncertain democracy
- one party rule
- military dictatorship
- monarchy / theocracy
- disordered or collapsed state (war)
- dependent territory

## Wars 1997–2001

Between 1997 and 2001 the country was involved in

- war with another state
- civil war
- intervention in another country's civil war
- a war of independence

# 4 Ethnicity

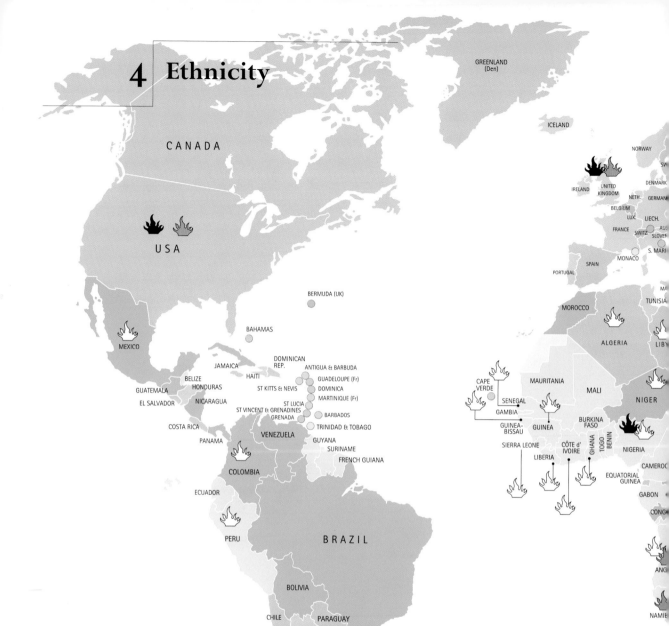

Viewed over the long term, peace between neighboring ethnic groups is statistically more common than war between them. But differences of ethnicity, race and nation offer rich opportunities to political leaders seeking to unite their followers on the most convenient basis – the fear of anybody who is different, the need to find a group of outsiders to blame for the things that are wrong with life. In the name of these fears and illusions, all over the world too many people are too willing to suspend rational argument, support violence against others, and accept restrictions on their own freedoms.

At the start of the 21st century, the majority of the most ethnically diverse countries were not at war. Nonetheless, the risk of war was higher in such countries, especially the ones that were also poor and undemocratic. In some cases, however, the ethnic diversity of the country has nothing to do with starting the war.

Where civil war was been justified on the basis of a threat from a different ethnic group, race or nation, mutual fear and hatred escalate along with the violence, making reconciliation seem a distant prospect. Then the risk of returning to warfare can be extremely high.

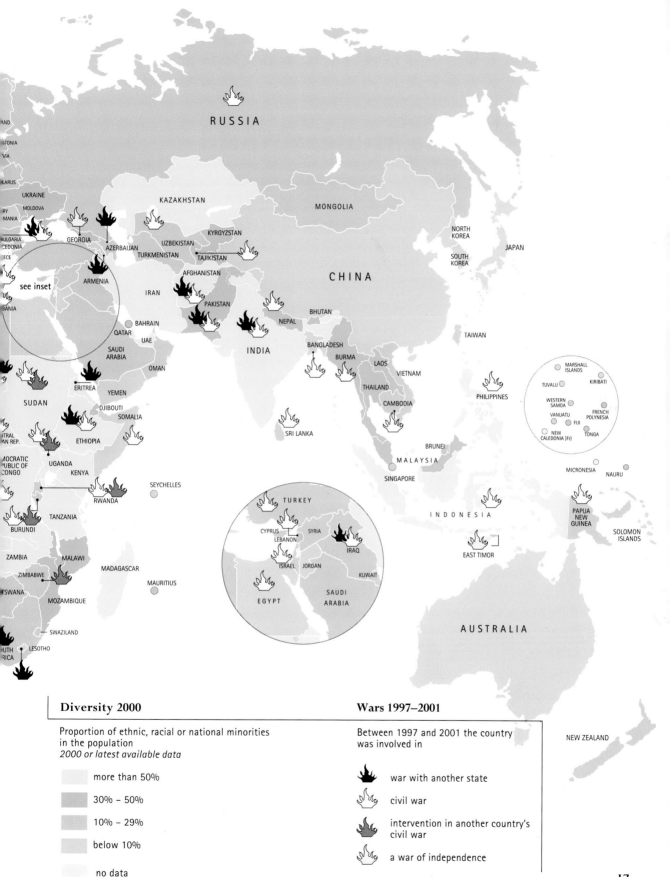

RUSSIA

UKRAINE
MOLDOVA
MANIA
BULGARIA
CEDONIA
EECE
ALBANIA
see inset

GEORGIA
AZERBAIJAN
ARMENIA

KAZAKHSTAN

UZBEKISTAN
TURKMENISTAN
KYRGYZSTAN
TAJIKISTAN

MONGOLIA

NORTH
KOREA
SOUTH
KOREA

JAPAN

IRAN
BAHRAIN
QATAR
UAE
SAUDI
ARABIA
OMAN
YEMEN

AFGHANISTAN
PAKISTAN

INDIA

NEPAL

BHUTAN

BANGLADESH
BURMA

CHINA

TAIWAN

LAOS
VIETNAM
THAILAND
CAMBODIA

PHILIPPINES

MARSHALL
ISLANDS
TUVALU
KIRIBATI
WESTERN
SAMOA
FRENCH
POLYNESIA
VANUATU
FIJI
NEW
CALEDONIA )Fr)
TONGA

ERITREA

SUDAN
DJIBOUTI
SOMALIA

SRI LANKA

BRUNEI

MALAYSIA

MICRONESIA
NAURU

TRAL
AN REP.
ETHIOPIA

MOCRATIC
UBLIC OF
CONGO
UGANDA
KENYA

SEYCHELLES

SINGAPORE

INDONESIA

PAPUA
NEW
GUINEA
SOLOMON
ISLANDS

RWANDA

BURUNDI
TANZANIA

ZAMBIA
MALAWI
ZIMBABWE
TSWANA
MOZAMBIQUE

MADAGASCAR

MAURITIUS

TURKEY
CYPRUS
LEBANON
SYRIA
ISRAEL
JORDAN
IRAQ
KUWAIT

EAST TIMOR

AUSTRALIA

EGYPT
SAUDI
ARABIA

SWAZILAND
UTH
RICA
LESOTHO

**Diversity 2000**

Proportion of ethnic, racial or national minorities
in the population
*2000 or latest available data*

more than 50%

30% – 50%

10% – 29%

below 10%

no data

**Wars 1997–2001**

Between 1997 and 2001 the country
was involved in

war with another state

civil war

intervention in another country's
civil war

a war of independence

NEW ZEALAND

17

# CHAPTER TWO

# The Military World

THE MILITARY WORLD TODAY has less to do with security than it has to do with power and the ability to project power.

The confrontation between the USA and the USSR from the end of World War Two until 1989 was always both political and military. While the military confrontation was heavily focused on Europe and northeast Asia, where enormous armed forces were concentrated, US-Soviet rivalry was always also global in scope.

But the Cold War was not ended by military means. It ended because the social and economic system in the Soviet bloc was not sustainable and, as it crumbled, the political system was unable to take the pressure and stabilise the situation.

## Major operational weapons systems worldwide

regional percentages and total numbers
*2002*

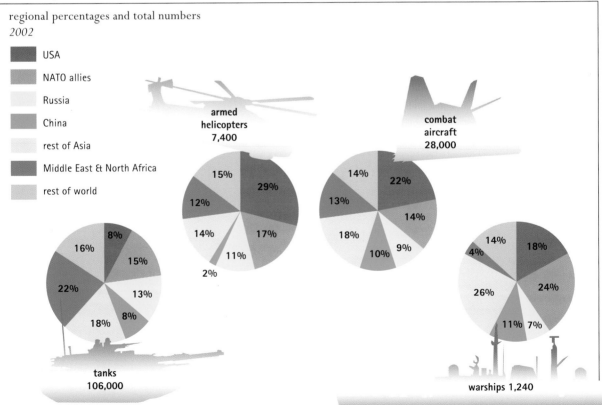

USA
NATO allies
Russia
China
rest of Asia
Middle East & North Africa
rest of world

armed helicopters
7,400

29% 17% 11% 2% 14% 12% 15%

combat aircraft
28,000

22% 14% 9% 10% 18% 13% 14%

tanks
106,000

8% 15% 13% 8% 18% 22% 16%

warships 1,240

18% 24% 7% 11% 26% 4% 14%

After all that military effort, it turned out that, at a deeper level, true security lay not in the strength of the armed forces but in the strength of a society, an economy and the political system.

As this truth sank in, it also occurred to many people that, even before the end of the Cold War, Europe had solved one of its major security problems and done so by largely non-military means. For over 70 years before World War Two, the dominant security problem in Europe was the rivalry between France and Germany. Today, war between them is unthinkable, not only because they are allies in NATO but more fundamentally because their futures are tied together in prosperous economic cooperation in the European Union.

Although the basis for security may be prosperity, democracy and cooperation, some aspects of security can only be provided by military means. In peacekeeping, for example (pages 106–13) armed forces can fulfil essential functions that cannot be carried out in any other way. But this does not create peace or security: rather, it keeps things under control until the foundations for true peace and security have been laid. Moreover, while security may be ultimately based on non-military means, it is still true that for the most powerful, armed force gives political power. There is no doubt which state is the most powerful.

The simple figures that show the USA's imposing ownership of military hardware actually understate its predominance. Many of the 80,000 battle tanks and 18,000 combat aircraft that the USA and its NATO allies do not own are badly maintained, prone to break down and only really operational about half the time. Even of fully maintained equipment, the USA has the newest and most advanced items. As a result, the USA – backed by its allies when it wants them there – can project force and therefore power to every part of the world.

But power is not security. The attack on the World Trade Center and the Pentagon on 11 September 2001 brought that fact home. In the days before the attack, America was deeply engaged in a discussion about anti-missile defence, a high-technology system for defence against the most advanced weapons in the world, a system that would be useless against the 11 September attacks.

Indeed, power and security can be contradictory to each other. It is the USA's global projection of power – not least in the Middle East, especially with its bases in Saudi Arabia – that has so enraged some political fanatics that they are apparently prepared to go to any lengths to attack the USA itself. If the USA wants to use its power to protect its interests in the Middle East, threats to the security and well being of Americans may be unavoidable in a small world. The military world is not everything.

# 5 | Under Arms

The world's regular armed forces and reserves consist of approximately 54 million men (mostly) and women, or a little less than one percent of the world population. This is about 10 percent fewer than in the mid-1980s, at the height of the Cold War. Regular armed forces alone amount to about 22 million, which is 20 percent less than in the mid-1980s.

The number of military personnel alone is a poor guide to military strength. Some armed forces pack a much heavier punch than much larger forces. There can be many reasons for this, among them the standard of training and organization within the military, whether it is committed to or

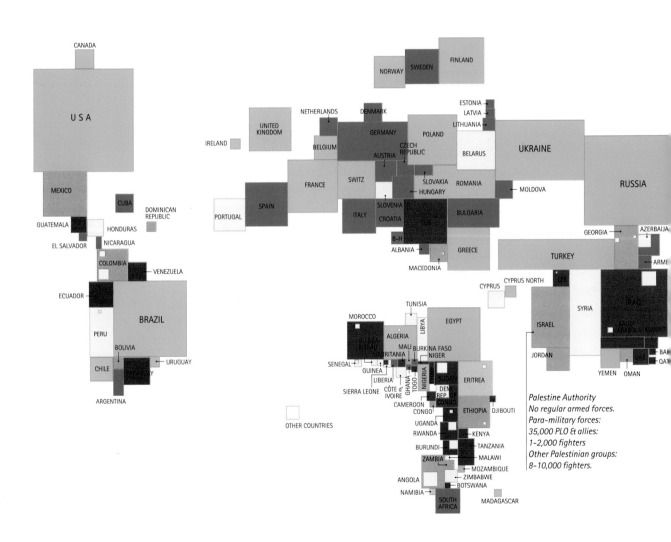

*Palestine Authority*
*No regular armed forces.*
*Para-military forces:*
*35,000 PLO & allies:*
*1–2,000 fighters*
*Other Palestinian groups:*
*8–10,000 fighters.*

alienated from the goals of the government, whether it has more advanced technology than its opponents.

Insurgent forces are usually quite small by comparison with the military personnel available to governments, especially if reserves are also mobilized. But the insurgents are often better trained, normally more committed and sometimes as well equipped as the government forces they are fighting.

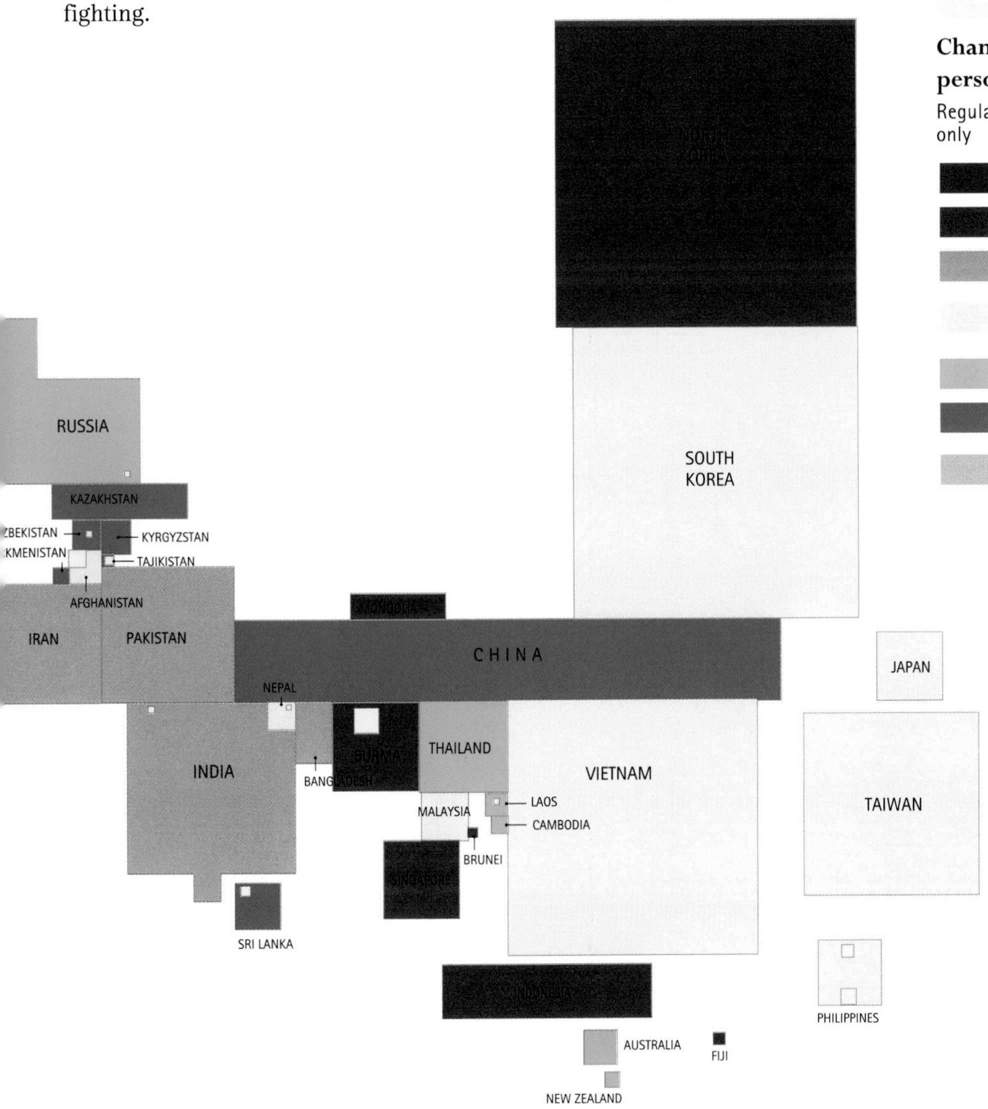

## World military personnel

Regular and reserve government forces and opposition forces

Percentage shares of world total *2001*

☐ =1%
☐ =0.1%
☐ =0.01%

☐ opposition forces
*where data exist*

## Change in number of military personnel *1985–2001*

Regular and reserve government forces only

■ increase of more than 100%

■ increase of 50%–100%

▨ increase of 10%–50%

☐ no change
*within 10% either way*

▨ decrease of 10%–50%

■ decrease of more than 50%

▨ comparison not possible

RUSSIA

KAZAKHSTAN

UZBEKISTAN — — KYRGYZSTAN
TURKMENISTAN — — TAJIKISTAN

AFGHANISTAN

NORTH KOREA

SOUTH KOREA

IRAN    PAKISTAN

MONGOLIA

CHINA

JAPAN

NEPAL

INDIA    BURMA    THAILAND    VIETNAM

BANGLADESH

MALAYSIA — LAOS
— CAMBODIA

BRUNEI

SINGAPORE

TAIWAN

SRI LANKA

INDONESIA

PHILIPPINES

AUSTRALIA    ■ FIJI

NEW ZEALAND

# 6 | Military Service

Most states treat military service by young men as a duty and force them to fulfil it, sometimes with a let out for reasons of conscience. Most states that only accept volunteers do so not because of the principle of individual freedom of choice, but because forces made up of professional volunteers are more efficient. The USA introduced an all-volunteer force in the 1970s after the Vietnam War, because of the belief that relying on unwilling drafted warriors would not work any more.

Professional terms of service are usually longer than compulsory terms so that professionals can be trained in more arduous

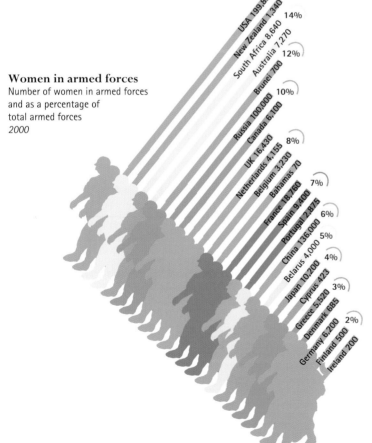

**Women in armed forces**
Number of women in armed forces and as a percentage of total armed forces
*2000*

USA 199,850 1,340 — 15%
New Zealand — 14%
South Africa 8,640
Australia 7,270 — 12%
Brunei 700
Russia 100,000 — 10%
Canada 6,100
UK 16,430 — 8%
Netherlands 4,155
Belgium 3,230
Bahamas 70
France 18,760 — 7%
Spain 9,400
Portugal 2,875 — 6%
China 136,000
Belarus 4,000 — 5%
Japan 10,200
Cyprus 423 — 4%
Greece 5,520
Denmark 685 — 3%
Germany 6,200
Finland 500 — 2%
Ireland 200

and complex tasks than their conscripted counterparts. They usually take more pride in their accomplishments along with a greater taste for fighting and more experience of combat.

The length of compulsory service for young men varies greatly. The initial service in Switzerland lasts for 15 weeks while in North Korea it can be as long as ten years. Within one country, the length of service is often different depending on whether the term is served in the army, navy or air force. Sometimes men from one ethnic group have

RUSSIA

NORWAY SWEDEN FINLAND

ESTONIA
LATVIA
LITHUANIA

UNITED DENMARK
KINGDOM
IRELAND
BELGIUM NETH. GERMANY POLAND BELARUS
LUX. CZECH SLO
FRANCE SWITZ. AUSTRIA HUNGARY MOLDOVA UKRAINE
CRO. B-H YUG ROMANIA
ITALY ALB. M.
BULGARIA GEORGIA

KAZAKHSTAN

MONGOLIA

PORTUGAL SPAIN
GREECE
MALTA
TURKEY

AZERBAIJAN
ARMENIA UZBEKISTAN KYRGYZSTAN
TURKMENISTAN TAJIKISTAN

NORTH
KOREA JAPAN
SOUTH
KOREA

MOROCCO TUNISIA
CYPRUS SYRIA
LEB IRAQ IRAN
ISRAEL
JORDAN AFGHANISTAN

CHINA

ALGERIA LIBYA EGYPT
KUWAIT BAHRAIN
QATAR UAE
SAUDI OMAN
ARABIA
PAKISTAN

NEPAL

TAIWAN

BANGLADESH

CAPE
VERDE MAURITANIA MALI
NIGER
ERITREA YEMEN

INDIA BURMA LAOS
VIETNAM
THAILAND
PHILIPPINES

SENEGAL
GAMBIA
GUINEA- BURKINA
BISSAU GUINEA FASO CHAD SUDAN
DJIBOUTI
CAMBODIA
SIERRA LEONE CÔTE d' NIGERIA
LIBERIA IVOIRE GHANA ETHIOPIA
TOGO BENIN CENTRAL
CAMEROON AFRICAN REPUBLIC

SRI LANKA

BRUNEI
MALAYSIA
SINGAPORE

EQUATORIAL
GUINEA DEMOCRATIC UGANDA
GABON REPUBLIC OF KENYA
CONGO CONGO
RWANDA
BURUNDI
TANZANIA

SEYCHELLES

I N D O N E S I A
PAPUA
NEW
GUINEA

ANGOLA

ZAMBIA MALAWI
ZIMBABWE MADAGASCAR
NAMIBIA
BOTSWANA
MOZAMBIQUE

AUSTRALIA

FIJI

SOUTH
AFRICA LESOTHO

NEW ZEALAND

**Length of compulsory
military service**

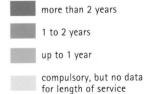

more than 2 years

1 to 2 years

up to 1 year

compulsory, but no data
for length of service

not compulsory

no data

to do longer service than those from
another.

In recent years, armed forces have slowly
started to overcome their reluctance to
employ women. Where they do, they
normally employ women mainly in
medicine, communications, administration
and other parts of the military
infrastructure, rather than in combat roles.
However, the USA is increasingly treating
women on equal terms with men and
allowing them into combat.

# 7 | Military Spending

World military spending in 2000 was US$810 billion annually. This was about one-third less than it had been at the height of the Cold War fifteen years earlier.

The end of the long East-West confrontation led to radical cuts in arms spending by most of the countries that were centrally involved in it, and left the USA in a position of military predominance, despite its own cuts.

How much is spent on the military is a result of decisions by a government about a variety of factors, ranging from the need for security to the desire for prestige at home and the urge for power in far-flung parts of the world.

There are many ways of measuring the economic burden these decisions produce. The coins show how the fifteen states with the largest military budgets compare to each other when it comes to military spending per person.

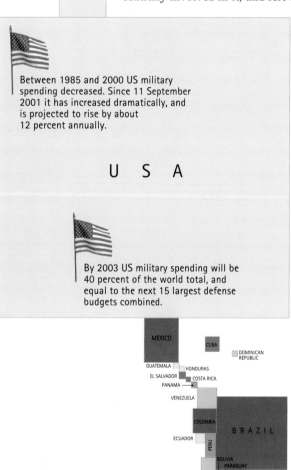

Between 1985 and 2000 US military spending decreased. Since 11 September 2001 it has increased dramatically, and is projected to rise by about 12 percent annually.

By 2003 US military spending will be 40 percent of the world total, and equal to the next 15 largest defense budgets combined.

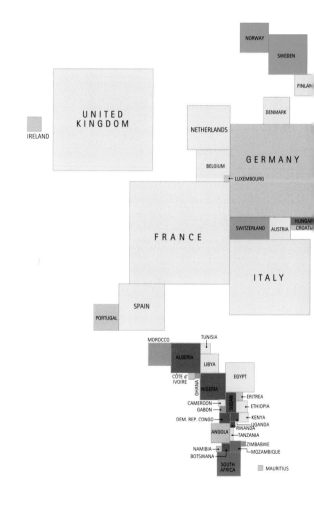

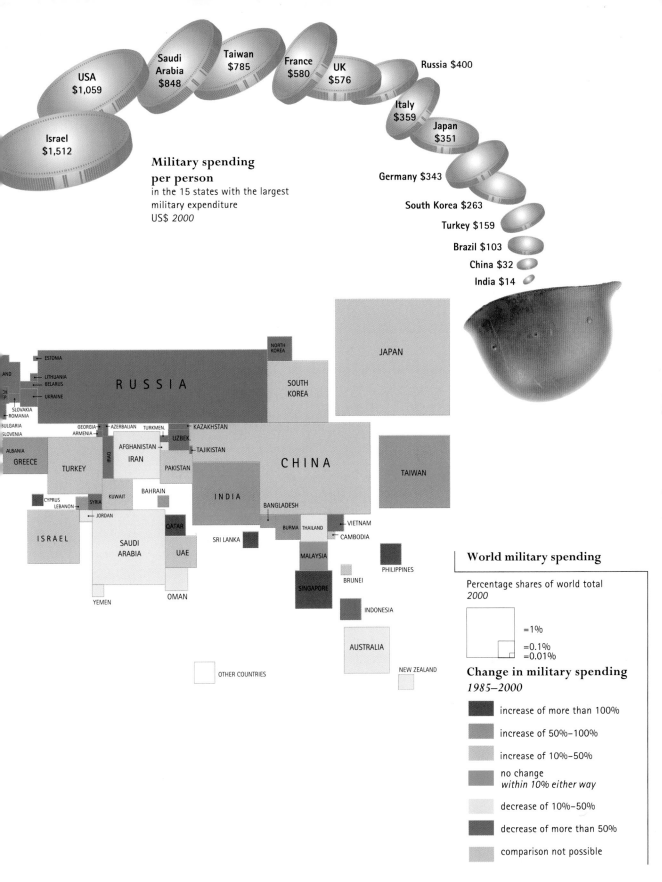

## Military spending per person
in the 15 states with the largest military expenditure
US$ *2000*

Israel $1,512
USA $1,059
Saudi Arabia $848
Taiwan $785
France $580
UK $576
Russia $400
Italy $359
Japan $351
Germany $343
South Korea $263
Turkey $159
Brazil $103
China $32
India $14

## World military spending

Percentage shares of world total
*2000*

☐ =1%
=0.1%
=0.01%

### Change in military spending
*1985–2000*

- increase of more than 100%
- increase of 50%–100%
- increase of 10%–50%
- no change *within 10% either way*
- decrease of 10%–50%
- decrease of more than 50%
- comparison not possible

25

# 8 | Mass Destruction

There are far fewer nuclear weapons now than there were at the height of the Cold War. Their destructive power remains unimaginable – one modestly sized nuclear weapon can destroy a major city. Many experts believe that the greatest risk of nuclear war is in the confrontation between the two smallest and newest nuclear powers – India and Pakistan.

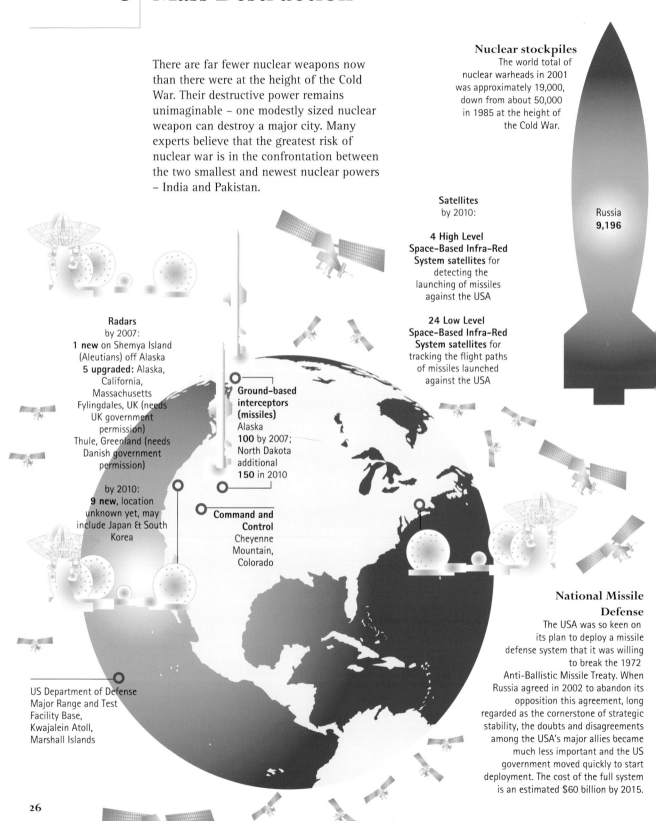

**Nuclear stockpiles**
The world total of nuclear warheads in 2001 was approximately 19,000, down from about 50,000 in 1985 at the height of the Cold War.

Russia
**9,196**

**Satellites**
by 2010:

**4 High Level Space-Based Infra-Red System satellites** for detecting the launching of missiles against the USA

**24 Low Level Space-Based Infra-Red System satellites** for tracking the flight paths of missiles launched against the USA

**Radars**
by 2007:
**1 new** on Shemya Island (Aleutians) off Alaska
**5 upgraded:** Alaska, California, Massachusetts
Fylingdales, UK (needs UK government permission)
Thule, Greenland (needs Danish government permission)

by 2010:
**9 new**, location unknown yet, may include Japan & South Korea

**Ground-based interceptors (missiles)**
Alaska
**100** by 2007;
North Dakota additional
**150** in 2010

**Command and Control**
Cheyenne Mountain, Colorado

US Department of Defense Major Range and Test Facility Base, Kwajalein Atoll, Marshall Islands

**National Missile Defense**
The USA was so keen on its plan to deploy a missile defense system that it was willing to break the 1972 Anti-Ballistic Missile Treaty. When Russia agreed in 2002 to abandon its opposition this agreement, long regarded as the cornerstone of strategic stability, the doubts and disagreements among the USA's major allies became much less important and the US government moved quickly to start deployment. The cost of the full system is an estimated $60 billion by 2015.

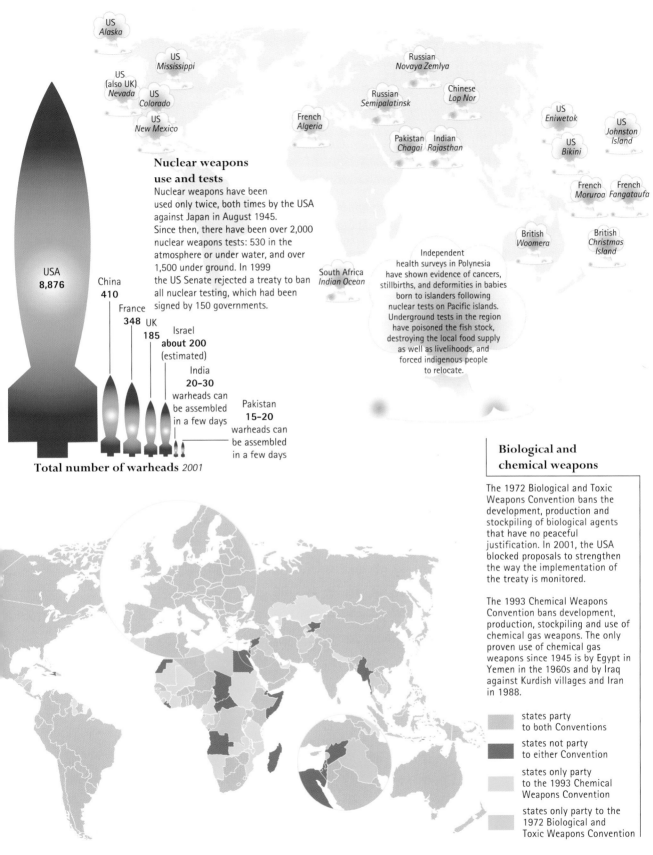

US
*Alaska*

US
*Mississippi*

US
(also UK)
*Nevada*

US
*Colorado*

US
*New Mexico*

Russian
*Novaya Zemlya*

Russian
*Semipalatinsk*

Chinese
*Lop Nor*

French
*Algeria*

Pakistan   Indian
*Chagai*  *Rajasthan*

US
*Eniwetok*

US
*Bikini*

US
*Johnston Island*

French   French
*Moruroa* *Fangataufa*

British
*Woomera*

British
*Christmas Island*

## Nuclear weapons use and tests

Nuclear weapons have been used only twice, both times by the USA against Japan in August 1945. Since then, there have been over 2,000 nuclear weapons tests: 530 in the atmosphere or under water, and over 1,500 under ground. In 1999 the US Senate rejected a treaty to ban all nuclear testing, which had been signed by 150 governments.

South Africa
*Indian Ocean*

Independent health surveys in Polynesia have shown evidence of cancers, stillbirths, and deformities in babies born to islanders following nuclear tests on Pacific islands. Underground tests in the region have poisoned the fish stock, destroying the local food supply as well as livelihoods, and forced indigenous people to relocate.

USA
**8,876**

China
**410**

France
**348**

UK
**185**

Israel
**about 200**
(estimated)

India
**20–30**
warheads can be assembled in a few days

Pakistan
**15–20**
warheads can be assembled in a few days

**Total number of warheads** *2001*

## Biological and chemical weapons

The 1972 Biological and Toxic Weapons Convention bans the development, production and stockpiling of biological agents that have no peaceful justification. In 2001, the USA blocked proposals to strengthen the way the implementation of the treaty is monitored.

The 1993 Chemical Weapons Convention bans development, production, stockpiling and use of chemical gas weapons. The only proven use of chemical gas weapons since 1945 is by Egypt in Yemen in the 1960s and by Iraq against Kurdish villages and Iran in 1988.

states party to both Conventions

states not party to either Convention

states only party to the 1993 Chemical Weapons Convention

states only party to the 1972 Biological and Toxic Weapons Convention

# 9 The International Arms Trade

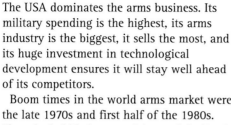

The USA dominates the arms business. Its military spending is the highest, its arms industry is the biggest, it sells the most, and its huge investment in technological development ensures it will stay well ahead of its competitors.

Boom times in the world arms market were the late 1970s and first half of the 1980s. Then the bubble burst and demand declined as the Cold War came to an end. In the second half of the 1990s, the market stabilised, but there has been no new boom.

There is serious concern about selling to some customers, either because they are especially repugnant or because they are involved in armed conflicts. So arms embargoes are often imposed.

Arms embargoes may restrict some tactical options, because spare parts and new equipment to repair or replace weapons lost in fighting are no longer available. Embargoes may also make it harder for a state to prepare for war.

But an embargo has never successfully stopped a war after it started. It is usually a way for supplier states to claim their hands are clean. And there is almost always a way round an embargo.

**Arms embargoes**

■ states subject to international arms embargo for any length of time during *1996–2000*

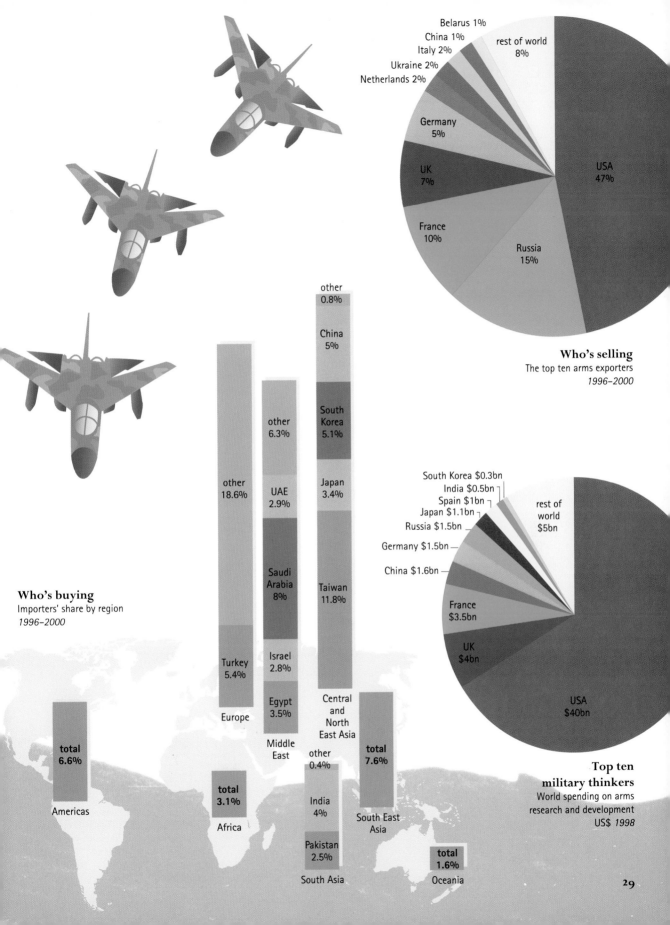

**Who's selling**
The top ten arms exporters
*1996–2000*

Belarus 1%
China 1%
Italy 2%
Ukraine 2%
Netherlands 2%
rest of world 8%
Germany 5%
UK 7%
France 10%
USA 47%
Russia 15%

**Who's buying**
Importers' share by region
*1996–2000*

**Europe**
other 18.6%
Turkey 5.4%

**Middle East**
other 6.3%
UAE 2.9%
Saudi Arabia 8%
Israel 2.8%
Egypt 3.5%

**Central and North East Asia**
other 0.8%
China 5%
South Korea 5.1%
Japan 3.4%
Taiwan 11.8%

**Americas**
total 6.6%

**Africa**
total 3.1%

**South Asia**
other 0.4%
India 4%
Pakistan 2.5%

**South East Asia**
total 7.6%

**Oceania**
total 1.6%

**Top ten military thinkers**
World spending on arms research and development
US$ *1998*

South Korea $0.3bn
India $0.5bn
Spain $1bn
Japan $1.1bn
Russia $1.5bn
Germany $1.5bn
China $1.6bn
France $3.5bn
UK $4bn
USA $40bn
rest of world $5bn

29

# Small Arms Trade

There is little reliable information about the scale of the global problem of small arms. Estimates indicate the following:

- 500 million small arms are available worldwide;
- annual trade in small arms worldwide amounts to US$5 billion;
- one-fifth of the total trade is illegal;
- 500,000 people are killed each year by small arms, of which about 200,000 are killed in crimes and about 300,000 in wars.

The availability of small arms does not provide the motive for war, but often the means. In 1997, chaos in Albania released thousands of weapons from the country's armed forces, many of which found their way to fighters in Kosovo next door. The collapse of the USSR in 1991 released huge numbers of weapons of all sizes into a zone stretching from the western shores of the Black Sea to Central Asia.

The problems created by the availability of small arms are often at their worst immediately after war rather than during it.

Peace means that there is suddenly a glut of weapons not being used. Guns are often sold cheaply – a Kalashnikov in good condition might raise about $20-$25 in cash, or food worth that much – and then sold again, either in another war zone, or to criminals. Weapons from Mozambique, where peace was agreed in 1992, found their way into the South African underworld and into the wars of central Africa.

Programs to buy back guns from the fighters are often counter-productive. Corruption is rife among those responsible for looking after the bought-back weapons; too often they sell them again for half the price, and keep the cash. In addition, the fact that there is a good market price attracts weapons from neighboring countries, which makes it hard to know exactly who is being disarmed by the buy-back program.

As long as small arms continue to be manufactured in such huge numbers, and as long as major producing countries have lax controls, the problem will persist.

## Small arms exporters
Top ten countries
US$ millions

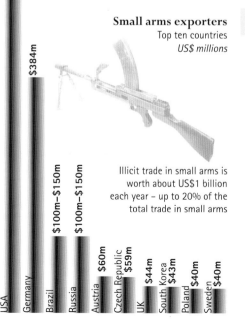

Illicit trade in small arms is worth about US$1 billion each year – up to 20% of the total trade in small arms

over $1,200m — USA
$384m — Germany
$100m–$150m — Brazil
$100m–$150m — Russia
$60m — Austria
$59m — Czech Republic
$44m — UK
$43m — South Korea
$40m — Poland
$40m — Sweden

## Mysterious ships

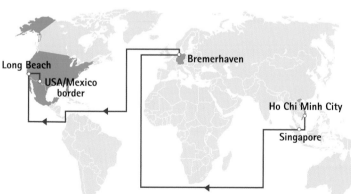

Long Beach
USA/Mexico border
Bremerhaven
Ho Chi Minh City
Singapore

**March 1997**
*Federal agents on the US-Mexico border opened two suspect sealed containers from Long Beach.*

*The arms had originally been left behind in Vietnam by the US armed forces. They had been shipped from Ho Chi Minh City*

*to Singapore, then to Bremerhaven in Germany, through the Panama Canal and up to Long Beach for transit to Mexico.*

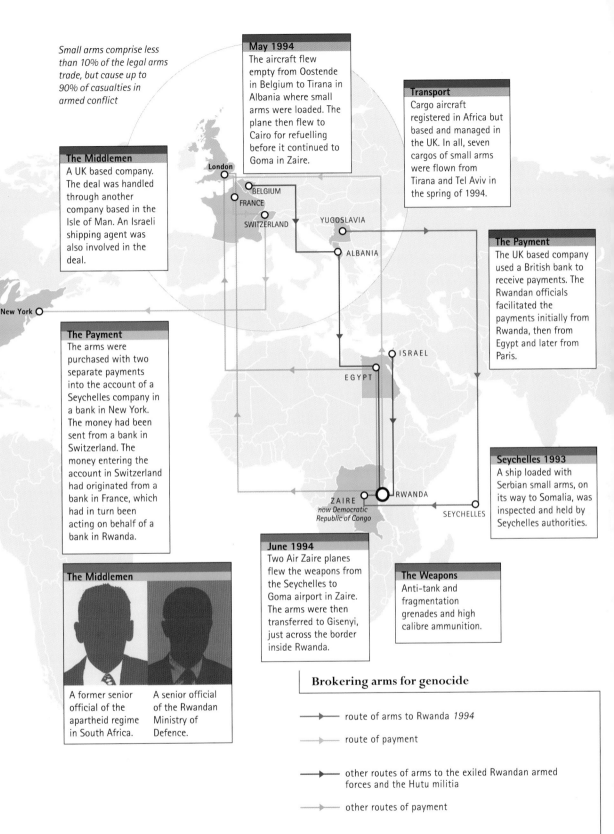

*Small arms comprise less than 10% of the legal arms trade, but cause up to 90% of casualties in armed conflict*

**May 1994**
The aircraft flew empty from Oostende in Belgium to Tirana in Albania where small arms were loaded. The plane then flew to Cairo for refuelling before it continued to Goma in Zaire.

**Transport**
Cargo aircraft registered in Africa but based and managed in the UK. In all, seven cargos of small arms were flown from Tirana and Tel Aviv in the spring of 1994.

**The Middlemen**
A UK based company. The deal was handled through another company based in the Isle of Man. An Israeli shipping agent was also involved in the deal.

**The Payment**
The UK based company used a British bank to receive payments. The Rwandan officials facilitated the payments initially from Rwanda, then from Egypt and later from Paris.

**The Payment**
The arms were purchased with two separate payments into the account of a Seychelles company in a bank in New York. The money had been sent from a bank in Switzerland. The money entering the account in Switzerland had originated from a bank in France, which had in turn been acting on behalf of a bank in Rwanda.

**Seychelles 1993**
A ship loaded with Serbian small arms, on its way to Somalia, was inspected and held by Seychelles authorities.

**June 1994**
Two Air Zaire planes flew the weapons from the Seychelles to Goma airport in Zaire. The arms were then transferred to Gisenyi, just across the border inside Rwanda.

**The Weapons**
Anti-tank and fragmentation grenades and high calibre ammunition.

**The Middlemen**

A former senior official of the apartheid regime in South Africa.

A senior official of the Rwandan Ministry of Defence.

London
BELGIUM
FRANCE
SWITZERLAND
YUGOSLAVIA
ALBANIA
New York
ISRAEL
EGYPT
ZAIRE
*now Democratic Republic of Congo*
RWANDA
SEYCHELLES

## Brokering arms for genocide

→ route of arms to Rwanda *1994*

→ route of payment

→ other routes of arms to the exiled Rwandan armed forces and the Hutu militia

→ other routes of payment

# 11 | Terrorism

Terrorism is usually the tactic of the force
that is weaker than its enemy. The weapons
of terrorism are assassinations of political
leaders and indiscriminate attacks on
civilians, usually with bombs.

USA

**New York and
Washington DC 2001
August 6** *According to
press reports, President
Bush was given an
intelligence briefing
predicting terrorist group
al Qaida planned to hijack
aircraft, probably to use in
attacks on the USA.*
**September 11** *World
Trade Center and Pentagon
hit by hijacked aircraft:
3,200 killed.*

PANAMA

COLOMBIA

PERU

SIERRA LEONE

GUINEA

LIBERIA

ARGENTINA

Discussion of terrorism is full of moral
outrage and fear because it is cloaked in
secrecy and attacks either ordinary citizens
or political leaders. Yet it is hard to see what
is more outrageous or frightening about a
bomb placed under a car or in a bus, than a
missile that comes out of the sky. War is hell
when it strikes, regardless of how it strikes.

In historical perspective, it is not only
rebels who have used terrorism. The term
was invented to describe a government
strategy of rule by terror, and state terrorism
has been as common as anti-state terrorism
for the last two centuries. Even today, when
use of the term is almost exclusively
reserved for insurrectionaries, the terrorist
tactic of assassination is used as much by
governments as against them.

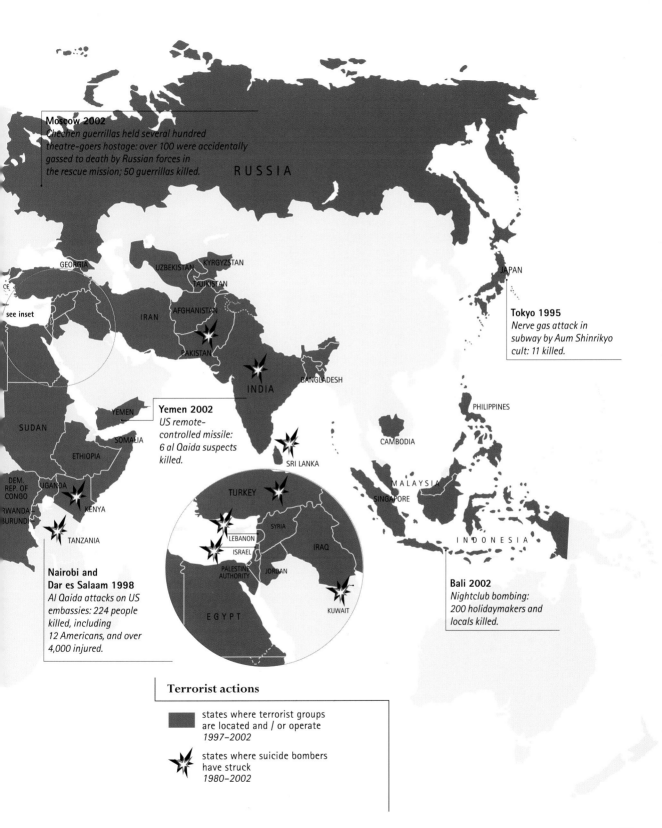

**Moscow 2002**
*Chechen guerrillas held several hundred theatre-goers hostage: over 100 were accidentally gassed to death by Russian forces in the rescue mission; 50 guerrillas killed.*

RUSSIA

GEORGIA   UZBEKISTAN   KYRGYZSTAN

CE          TAJIKISTAN

see inset   IRAN   AFGHANISTAN

PAKISTAN

BANGLADESH

INDIA

**Tokyo 1995**
*Nerve gas attack in subway by Aum Shinrikyo cult: 11 killed.*

JAPAN

PHILIPPINES

**Yemen 2002**
*US remote-controlled missile: 6 al Qaida suspects killed.*

YEMEN

SOMALIA

SUDAN

ETHIOPIA

SRI LANKA

CAMBODIA

MALAYSIA

SINGAPORE

DEM. REP. OF CONGO

UGANDA

RWANDA

BURUNDI

KENYA

TANZANIA

INDONESIA

**Nairobi and Dar es Salaam 1998**
*Al Qaida attacks on US embassies: 224 people killed, including 12 Americans, and over 4,000 injured.*

TURKEY

SYRIA

LEBANON

ISRAEL

IRAQ

PALESTINE AUTHORITY

JORDAN

EGYPT

KUWAIT

**Bali 2002**
*Nightclub bombing: 200 holidaymakers and locals killed.*

## Terrorist actions

states where terrorist groups are located and / or operate
*1997–2002*

states where suicide bombers have struck
*1980–2002*

# 12 | US Power

The mobilization of American defense and security measures after the terrorist attacks of September 11, 2001 led to increased military spending and expanded worldwide military presence. US forces returned to the Philippines, increased their numbers in the Gulf region of the Middle East, and deployed in Afghanistan and Central Asia for the first time. Military spending showed a one-year rise of 12 percent, building on earlier budget rises for a nearly 30 percent increase compared to 1998.

Coming at the same time as the Bush administration's tax cuts, rising military spending turned a budget surplus in 2000 into a budget deficit in 2002, reminiscent of the military spending booms during the Vietnam War in the 1960s, and the renewed Cold War of the 1980s.

The September 11 attacks had negative impacts on business and the economy, and these coincided with an already unfolding recession as the 1990s boom came to its inevitable end. Among the combined consequences was an increase in US poverty levels – small, it is true, but the first rise in poverty figures for a decade.

A year after the destruction of the World Trade Center, the US government voiced its new doctrine of pre-emptive action against security threats. Jettisoning the deterrence approach that had served successive US administrations for fifty years, the USA opted for a new but equally flawed approach. If deterrence theory is flawed because it depends on the rationality of both parties in crises, when rational judgement may be in short supply, pre-emptive strike theory is flawed because it means heavy reliance on the hazy information and uncertain estimates of the world of intelligence agencies.

Behind the US worldwide presence lies its need for oil. US oil consumption is 25 percent of the world total, and it imports 60 percent (and rising) of its requirements, much of it from the Middle East. Compared with new weapons and a new doctrine, a greater gain in security lies in a new pattern of energy consumption.

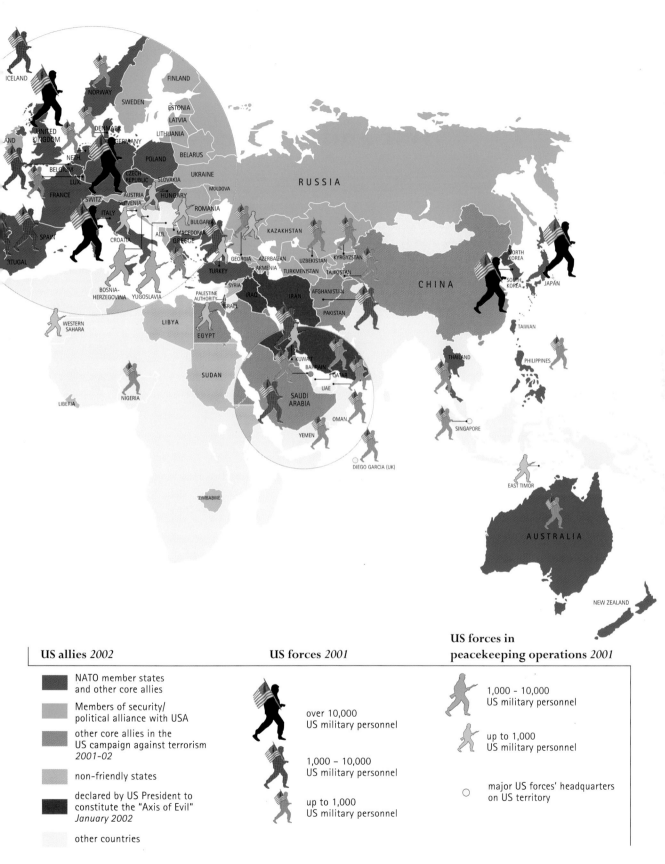

**US allies** *2002*

**NATO member states and other core allies**

Members of security/ political alliance with USA

other core allies in the US campaign against terrorism 2001-02

non-friendly states

declared by US President to constitute the "Axis of Evil" *January 2002*

other countries

**US forces** *2001*

over 10,000 US military personnel

1,000 – 10,000 US military personnel

up to 1,000 US military personnel

**US forces in peacekeeping operations** *2001*

1,000 – 10,000 US military personnel

up to 1,000 US military personnel

major US forces' headquarters on US territory

Map labels: ICELAND, NORWAY, SWEDEN, FINLAND, ESTONIA, LATVIA, LITHUANIA, UNITED KINGDOM, DENMARK, GERMANY, BELARUS, POLAND, NETH., BELGIUM, LUX., CZECH REPUBLIC, SLOVAKIA, UKRAINE, FRANCE, AUSTRIA, HUNGARY, MOLDOVA, SWITZ, SLOVENIA, ROMANIA, ITALY, CROATIA, BULGARIA, ALB., MACEDONIA, GREECE, SPAIN, PORTUGAL, BOSNIA-HERZEGOVINA, YUGOSLAVIA, WESTERN SAHARA, LIBERIA, NIGERIA, LIBYA, EGYPT, SUDAN, ZIMBABWE, PALESTINE AUTHORITY, ISRAEL, SYRIA, IRAQ, IRAN, TURKEY, GEORGIA, ARMENIA, AZERBAIJAN, TURKMENISTAN, UZBEKISTAN, KYRGYZSTAN, TAJIKISTAN, AFGHANISTAN, PAKISTAN, KAZAKHSTAN, RUSSIA, CHINA, NORTH KOREA, SOUTH KOREA, JAPAN, TAIWAN, THAILAND, PHILIPPINES, SINGAPORE, KUWAIT, BAHRAIN, QATAR, UAE, SAUDI ARABIA, OMAN, YEMEN, DIEGO GARCIA (UK), EAST TIMOR, AUSTRALIA, NEW ZEALAND

35

# CHAPTER THREE

# War and People

WAR IS HELL, said US General William Sherman, the man who ordered the burning of Atlanta in the American Civil War. But most people recognise an atrocity when they see or read about one – an act of war that is even more hellish than usual.

For in the hell of war, there are the laws of war or, as they are now called, international humanitarian law. These govern when it is right to fight, and how it is acceptable to fight. They are intended to limit the suffering of people and the damage to property in war. International humanitarian law shares with international human rights the goal of restricting the power of states and upholding the rights of the individual. But humanitarian law only covers wartime and only covers how force is used; whether and when a state has the right to use armed force are governed by the United Nations' Charter.

According to the UN Charter, states can use force in self-defence, for internal security or in actions that are authorized by the UN Security Council and are intended to restore peace and safety after war has broken out.

According to the law, if war does break out, those not taking part in the fighting should be protected. That includes civilians, medical personnel, and those who were fighting but are not any more – the sick, the wounded, the shipwrecked and prisoners of war.

Humanitarian law also rules out the use of some weapons – some that cause unnecessary harm, some that are by their nature indiscriminate – and bans various military tactics and actions:

• It is not permitted to execute, starve or torture prisoners;
• It is not permitted to block or delay the work of medical personnel – for example, ambulances must be given safe passage;
• The military may not shoot at unarmed civilians with live ammunition, or shell or bomb the places where they are hiding;
• Nor is it permitted to use civilians as human shields against enemy attack;
• It is forbidden to use weapons or tactics that cause excessive suffering and unnecessary loss of life;
• Rape in war – or organising systematic rape – is a war crime;
• Looting and wanton destruction of property are also banned.

Under humanitarian law:
• Civilians must be given a reasonable chance to leave safely from places where fighting is going on;
• Proper medical care must be given to the sick and the wounded;
• Prisoners of war are to be given shelter and food as well as medical care, and they must be treated with dignity;

**Signing up for the International Criminal Court**

The 1998 statute establishing the ICC
*status at May 2002*

 ratified

 signed but not ratified

 neither signed nor ratified

• Every effort must be made to spare the lives of civilians, and to protect them from the effects of war;

• States must teach humanitarian law to their armed forces and to their citizens in general, and make all relevant information accessible to the public;

• States must enforce humanitarian law – when their own military personnel break it, when military personnel of other states break it and when political leaders break it.

Nevertheless these rules are continually broken and ignored.

The UN Security Council established two International Criminal Tribunals in the 1990s – one to deal with war crimes in the territory of the former Yugoslavia since 1991, and the other to deal with genocide and other serious crimes committed during 1994 in Rwanda (or by Rwandans in neighbouring countries). Both tribunals work slowly and face many obstacles. The biggest problem for the tribunal on Yugoslavia has been to arrest the suspects; for the tribunal on Rwanda, it has been that there are so many suspects – over 100,000.

In July 1998, agreement was reached in Rome to establish a permanent International Criminal Court to try crimes of genocide, war crimes and crimes against humanity. Four years later, enough states had ratified the "Rome Statute" for the new court to get ready to start work in The Hague. The USA, Russia and China are among those that have not ratified the agreement. The USA threatened to block further UN peacekeeping operations unless its forces were exempted from the Court's jurisdiction.

# 13 | Deaths

Among all the facts that are known about war today, one thing we do not know is how many people are killed.

A reasonable estimate for the number of people killed by war between 1997 and 2002 is just over three million. This is about two and a half million fewer war deaths than in the first half of the 1990s.

Approximately 75 percent of those killed in wars today are civilians. This figure is something between a guess and an estimate, because while military forces and guerrilla groups generally know how many of their fighters are dying in a war, there is in most wars no agency or organization whose job it is to count civilian deaths.

There are no reliable figures for numbers of people who are wounded in war. There are no figures for how many people suffer severe psychological damage. There are no figures for grief at the death of loved ones.

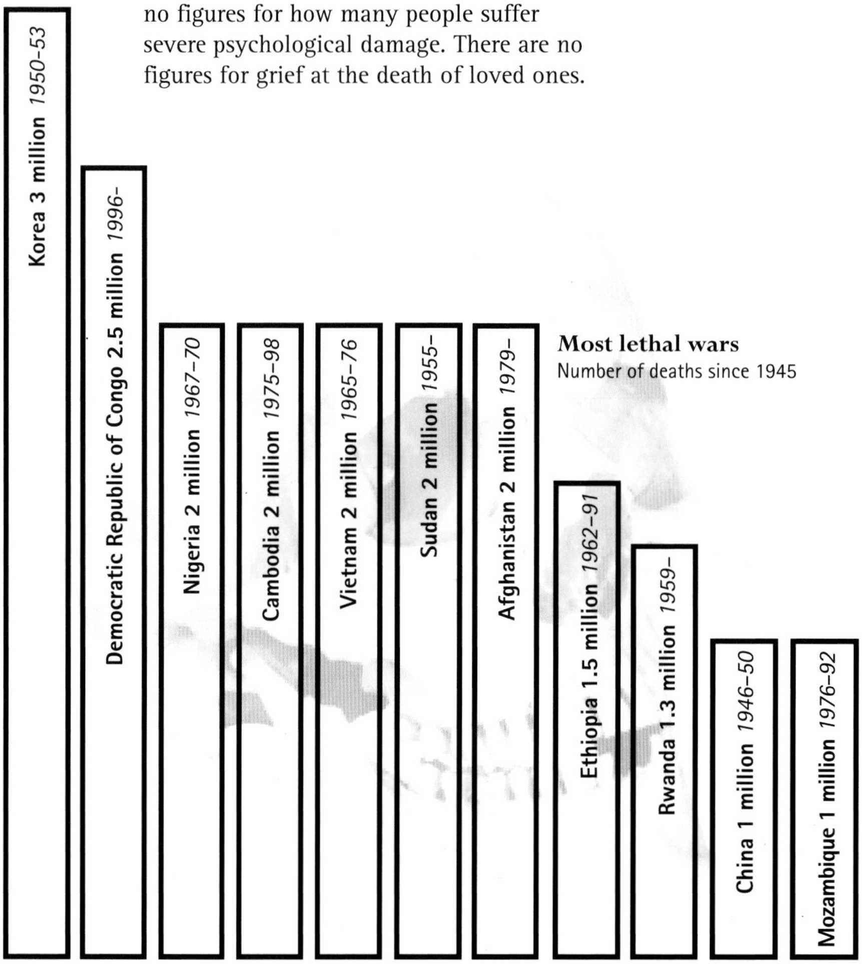

USA

MEXICO

COLOMBIA

PERU

**Most lethal wars**
Number of deaths since 1945

Korea 3 million *1950–53*

Democratic Republic of Congo 2.5 million *1996–*

Nigeria 2 million *1967–70*

Cambodia 2 million *1975–98*

Vietnam 2 million *1965–76*

Sudan 2 million *1955–*

Afghanistan 2 million *1979–*

Ethiopia 1.5 million *1962–91*

Rwanda 1.3 million *1959–*

China 1 million *1946–50*

Mozambique 1 million *1976–92*

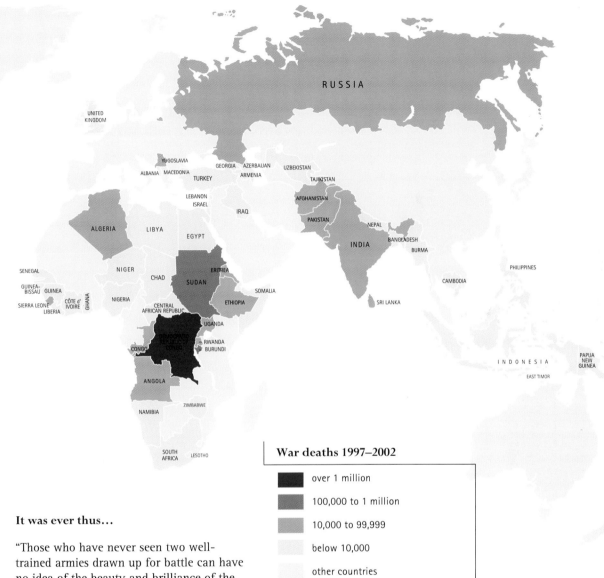

RUSSIA

UNITED KINGDOM

YUGOSLAVIA
ALBANIA  MACEDONIA
GEORGIA  AZERBAIJAN
UZBEKISTAN
ARMENIA
TURKEY
TAJIKISTAN
AFGHANISTAN
LEBANON
ISRAEL
IRAQ
PAKISTAN
NEPAL

ALGERIA  LIBYA
EGYPT
INDIA  BANGLADESH
BURMA

SENEGAL
NIGER
CHAD
ERITREA
SUDAN
GUINEA-BISSAU  GUINEA
SOMALIA
SIERRA LEONE  CÔTE d' IVOIRE  GHANA
NIGERIA
CENTRAL AFRICAN REPUBLIC
ETHIOPIA
LIBERIA
PHILIPPINES

CAMBODIA

SRI LANKA

UGANDA
DEMOCRATIC REPUBLIC OF CONGO
RWANDA
CONGO
BURUNDI
INDONESIA
PAPUA NEW GUINEA

ANGOLA
EAST TIMOR

NAMIBIA  ZIMBABWE

SOUTH AFRICA  LESOTHO

## War deaths 1997–2002

- over 1 million
- 100,000 to 1 million
- 10,000 to 99,999
- below 10,000
- other countries

The map shows war deaths only for the years 1997–2002. Some of the wars going on then had started years earlier. The map does not show the total deaths in those wars.

## It was ever thus…

"Those who have never seen two well-trained armies drawn up for battle can have no idea of the beauty and brilliance of the display. Bugles, fifes, oboes, drums and salvoes of artillery produced such a harmony as Hell itself could not rival. The opening barrage destroyed about six thousand men on each side. Rifle-fire which followed rid this best of worlds of about nine or ten thousand villains who infested its surface. Finally, the bayonet provided sufficient reason for the death of several thousand more. The total casualties amounted to about thirty thousand …

When all was over and the rival kings were celebrating their victory …"

Voltaire, *Candide* 1758

# 14 | Atrocities

**Northern Ireland 1972**

British troops opened fire and killed 14 civil rights protestors at a peaceful demonstration. An official enquiry in 1972 exonerated the soldiers, saying they had come under fire. Many testimonies dispute this. A new enquiry was opened in 1998.

**New York and the Pentagon, USA 2001**

Over 3,000 civilians of 80 nationalities were killed when passenger aircraft were deliberately crashed into the two towers of the World Trade Center in New York and the Pentagon.

**Bosnia–Herzegovina 1992–95**

Serbian forces used massacre, terror and rape for "ethnic cleansing" of large areas of the multi-ethnic republic. Later Bosniak and Bosnian Croatian forces also committed atrocities. In the worst single incident, Bosnian Serb forces killed over 7,000 Bosniak males in the small town of Srebrenica in June 1995.

**Colombia**

Reports from the BBC World Service: "Working on the principle that draining the water will kill the fish, the paramilitaries have provoked massive displacement through their policy of massacres and terror... The death squads arrive in communities in areas of guerrilla influence with a list in hand. The list contains names of suspected guerrilla sympathisers. All those on the list are killed, usually in front of their families and in a most gruesome manner." (January 7, 2002) "Left-wing rebels in Colombia have admitted firing a home-made mortar bomb at a church which killed up to 117 civilians..." (May 8, 2002)

**Mexico 1997**

In the state of Chiapas, right-wing paramilitaries who seemed to have implicit army support shot and killed seven men, 20 women and 18 children – all of the Tzotzil indigenous group.

**Guatemala 1982**

In one of many massacres of civilians in the 36-year war in Guatemala, army soldiers and paramilitaries attacked the community of Rio Negro, killing 107 children and 70 women. This was the third of five massacres carried out against this one community, well known for opposing the internationally funded Chixoy Dam project; after the fifth massacre, the villagers' land was flooded.

**Peru 1980–99**

In a total of over 30,000 war deaths, over 80 percent were civilians. Government and insurgent forces were responsible for, respectively, just over half and just under half of the known cases of torture, disappearance, execution, and assassination.

**Sierra Leone 1992–2002**

To terrorize civilians, the Revolutionary United Front and other armed groups in Sierra Leone raped women and cut the limbs off men, women and children. They made civilians into slaves and children into soldiers.

**Algeria 1997**

In a single four hour incident on the outskirts of Algiers, over 300 people – mostly pregnant women, babies and the elderly – were killed, disembowelled and burned, and 40 girls and women were kidnapped, raped and subsequently murdered. Government and insurgents blamed each other.

Some acts shock the conscience of ordinary people and dispel the casual thought that in war, anything goes. Such acts are normally labelled atrocities. They break the limits of what is thought to be acceptable. Sometimes they are called atrocities because of the scale of suffering that they cause, sometimes because of the planned and careful cruelty that characterizes them, sometimes simply because they are unexpected. The map shows some that have shocked the world's conscience in the last three decades – and a few that should have.

## Hama, Syria 1982

To end an armed uprising, Syrian forces besieged the town of Hama, completely destroying one third of it and killing 30,000 to 40,000 civilians, about 10 percent of the town's population.

## Chechnya, Russia 1994–96 and since 1999

In the two wars in Chechnya, Russian forces have arrested large numbers of Chechen males on suspicion of terrorist activity; many have never been seen again. In 1999-2000, there were over 120 documented cases of summary execution. Bombing and shelling have destroyed most of the capital, Grozny. Looting of villages by Russian soldiers is common. Several thousand civilians have been killed.

## Western Burma 1991–92

The Burmese military dictatorship used forced labour, starvation, systematic rape and religious persecution to drive more than 250,000 people of the Rohingyas to seek refuge across the border in Bangladesh, which immediately arranged to return them to Burma.

## Halabja, Iraq 1988

Iraqi forces used mustard gas and nerve gas in attacking the Kurdish village of Halabja, killing at least 5,000 people. Iraqi forces also used chemical warfare against Iranian forces and other Kurdish villages in the late 1980s.

## Cambodia 1975-79

1.6 million people – about 20 percent of the population – were killed or starved to death during the Khmer Rouge's four year attempt to reconstruct Cambodia as a society without towns, without traditions, without families and without ideas, thoughts or feelings except those approved by the Khmer Rouge itself.

## Israel

**1953:** Qibya: In retaliation for the murder of an Israeli woman and her two children, Israeli Commando Unit 101 attacked the village of Qibya. It blew up 45 houses and killed 69 civilians, of whom 46 were women and children. Unit 101's commanding officer was Ariel Sharon.

**1982:** Beirut: Israeli army commanders were ordered to allow Lebanese Phalangist militia into Sabra and Chatilla refugee camps to expel Palestinian guerrillas reportedly hiding there. The number of civilians killed was between 800 and 2,000. The order to let the militia in was given by Israeli Defence Minister Ariel Sharon.

**2002:** As Israel hunted leaders of the Palestinian suicide bombers, Prime Minister Sharon praised as "a great success" a missile attack on a Gaza apartment block that killed a Palestinian militant leader, five other adults and ten children.

## Rwanda April-June 1994

Extremists in the Hutu government organised a massacre of the minority Tutsis and of Hutu opponents. The preparations were more detailed and larger scale than in previous massacres of Tutsis in the 1960s. In a six week period, specially trained army units and the militia killed 800,000 people; guns, axes, machetes, fire and burial alive were the commonest instruments of death. Practically every Tutsi female over the age of 12 who survived the genocide was raped. The Tutsi insurgents of the Rwandan Patriotic Front took power and ended the massacres, while the perpetrators joined the hundreds of thousands of Hutu refugees in camps in Zaire.

## Aceh, Indonesia 1989–98

Hundreds of corpses of civilians have been discovered in mass graves since 1998. Estimates put the number of missing people as high as 39,000. The worst period of massacres was 1989-1992. There is no definitive figure for the total killed by the Indonesian military.

## East Timor 1975 and 1999

Indonesia invaded the former Portuguese colony in 1975, taking control through terror and massacres of about 80,000 civilians. Just before conceding independence in 1999, Indonesian-trained militias killed up to 2,000 civilians, and forced two-thirds of the population from their homes.

# 15 Refugees

At the end of the 20th century approximately 40 million people had fled their homes for fear of war and persecution. Of these, just over 14 million have fled abroad, thus fulfilling the international definition of "refugee". At least six million live in a state of limbo, neither legally recognised as refugees, nor able to return home. About 20 million have found refuge inside their own countries: they may not have suffered less than the others, but they are likely to return home more quickly.

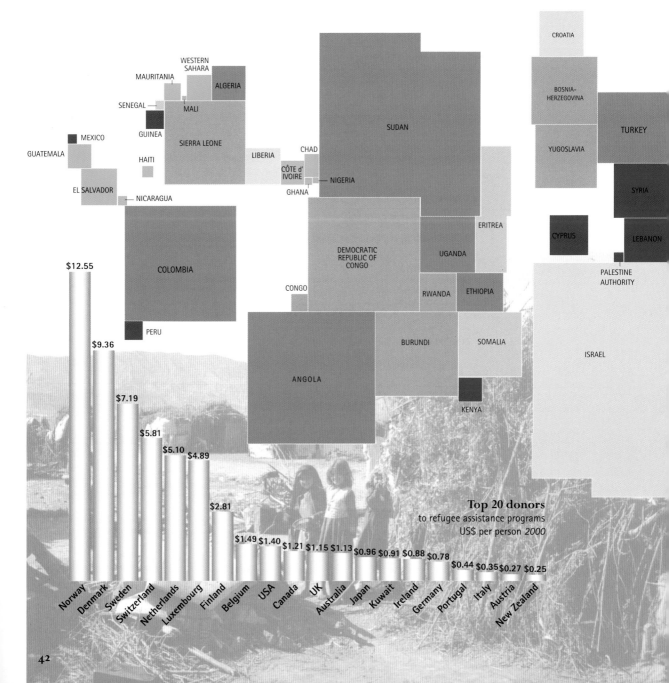

Top 20 donors
to refugee assistance programs
US$ per person *2000*

$12.55 Norway
$9.36 Denmark
$7.19 Sweden
$5.81 Switzerland
$5.10 Netherlands
$4.89 Luxembourg
$2.81 Finland
$1.49 Belgium
$1.40 USA
$1.21 Canada
$1.15 UK
$1.13 Australia
$0.96 Japan
$0.91 Kuwait
$0.88 Ireland
$0.78 Germany
$0.44 Portugal
$0.35 Italy
$0.27 Austria
$0.25 New Zealand

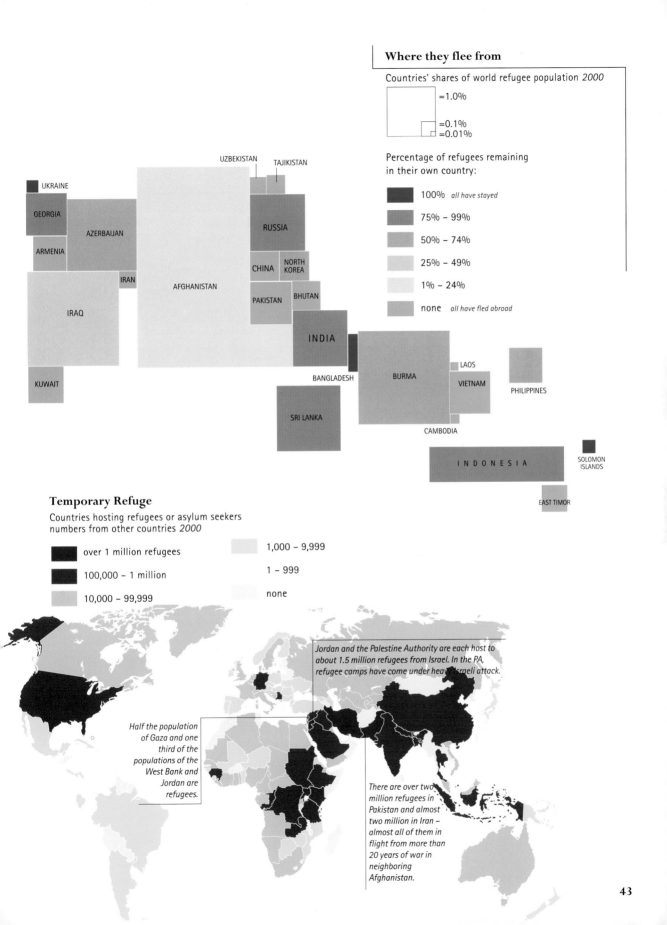

## Where they flee from

Countries' shares of world refugee population *2000*

= 1.0%
= 0.1%
= 0.01%

Percentage of refugees remaining
in their own country:

100% *all have stayed*
75% – 99%
50% – 74%
25% – 49%
1% – 24%
none *all have fled abroad*

UKRAINE
UZBEKISTAN
TAJIKISTAN
GEORGIA
AZERBAIJAN
RUSSIA
ARMENIA
CHINA
NORTH KOREA
IRAN
AFGHANISTAN
PAKISTAN
BHUTAN
IRAQ
INDIA
KUWAIT
BANGLADESH
SRI LANKA
BURMA
LAOS
VIETNAM
PHILIPPINES
CAMBODIA
INDONESIA
SOLOMON ISLANDS
EAST TIMOR

## Temporary Refuge

Countries hosting refugees or asylum seekers
numbers from other countries *2000*

over 1 million refugees
100,000 – 1 million
10,000 – 99,999
1,000 – 9,999
1 – 999
none

*Jordan and the Palestine Authority are each host to
about 1.5 million refugees from Israel. In the PA,
refugee camps have come under heavy Israeli attack.*

*Half the population
of Gaza and one
third of the
populations of the
West Bank and
Jordan are
refugees.*

*There are over two
million refugees in
Pakistan and almost
two million in Iran –
almost all of them in
flight from more than
20 years of war in
neighboring
Afghanistan.*

43

# 16 Landmines

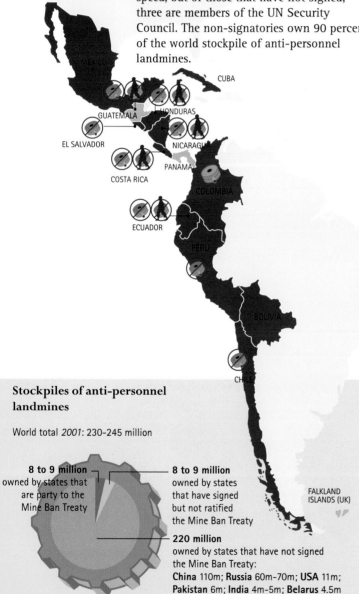

Each year, nearly 20,000 people are casualties of landmines and unexploded bombs and shells.

Since the Mine Ban Treaty was signed in 1997, the production of anti-personnel landmines has fallen dramatically – 41 states have stopped making them – and mine-clearance programs have grown. States have joined up to the Treaty at unprecedented speed, but of those that have not signed, three are members of the UN Security Council. The non-signatories own 90 percent of the world stockpile of anti-personnel landmines.

## Mine-affected countries and territories

Landmines and unexploded ordnance (UXOs)
*2000 – 2001*

- ■ casualties caused by landmines and UXOs
- ▨ landmines and UXOs present no casualties reported
- □ other countries

- 🚶 humanitarian mine-clearance program *1998-2001*
- ⊘ other mine-clearance program *1998-2001*

Use of anti-personnel landmines *2001-02*

-  by both government and rebel forces
-  by government forces
-  by rebel forces

## Stockpiles of anti-personnel landmines

World total *2001*: 230-245 million

**8 to 9 million**
owned by states that are party to the Mine Ban Treaty

**8 to 9 million**
owned by states that have signed but not ratified the Mine Ban Treaty

**220 million**
owned by states that have not signed the Mine Ban Treaty:
**China** 110m; **Russia** 60m-70m; **USA** 11m; **Pakistan** 6m; **India** 4m-5m; **Belarus** 4.5m

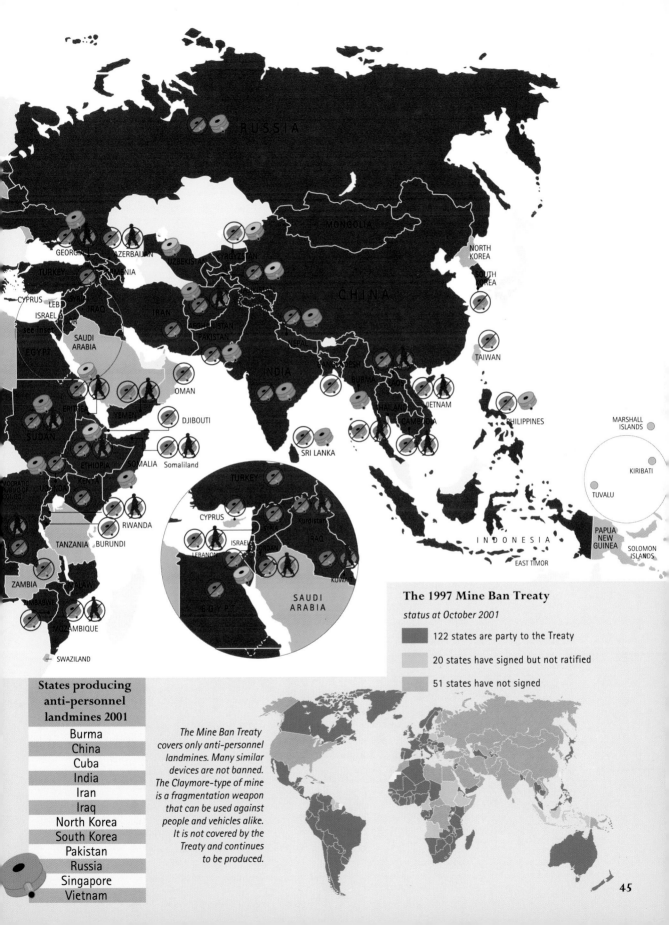

**The 1997 Mine Ban Treaty**

*status at October 2001*

122 states are party to the Treaty

20 states have signed but not ratified

51 states have not signed

**States producing anti-personnel landmines 2001**

| |
|---|
| Burma |
| China |
| Cuba |
| India |
| Iran |
| Iraq |
| North Korea |
| South Korea |
| Pakistan |
| Russia |
| Singapore |
| Vietnam |

*The Mine Ban Treaty covers only anti-personnel landmines. Many similar devices are not banned. The Claymore-type of mine is a fragmentation weapon that can be used against people and vehicles alike. It is not covered by the Treaty and continues to be produced.*

45

# 17 | Young Soldiers

Over 300,000 people below the age of 18 are fighting in wars around the world. Most of these young soldiers are between 15 and 18 years old, but there are many cases of children below the age of 15 being recruited and used as fighters.

Children can kill because modern small arms are light and easy to use. Children are recruited because they are cheap, expendable and easier to mould into unthinking killing and acceptance of danger.

Recruitment is often accomplished by force. There are well documented cases in which credible threats of killing or cutting off a limb have been used, and others in which torture was the means. Such child recruits are then usually asked to commit an act of brutality – such as killing one of their parents or an unwilling recruit – in order to blood them and psychologically numb them. Other children join armed groups in search of safety, and sometimes seek revenge.

Child soldiers live in a world of brutality inflicted by them and on them. Punishments are extreme and life is short. Many are sexually abused. Girls are recruited as well as boys. The girls are not often front-line fighters, although Sri Lanka, Colombia and Burundi are among the exceptions; duties usually combine sexual slavery with various military functions such as cooking, cleaning and looting.

In many cases, after their first blooding, child soldiers live in a semi-stupor induced by drugs and alcohol liberally provided by their commanders as a matter of policy. It reduces their sensitivity to the violence they inflict and suffer, and they do as they are told partly so they can keep feeding their growing, multiple addictions. The prestige that comes with a gun, a bottle of vodka and a murderous reputation is also part of the incentive.

When peace arrives, the trauma of war is replaced by disorientation. It is not easy to reintegrate hardened fighters of any age back into peaceful civil society; with fighters

In Bolivia almost half the armed forces are aged 14 to 17.

who are children, or who were recruited as children, the problem is worse.

Child soldiers have lost their homes, their upbringing, education, moral sense and opportunities for normal social development. Returning home may not be possible because home has been destroyed, or because of psychological disturbance created by what they have done and seen. Their physical

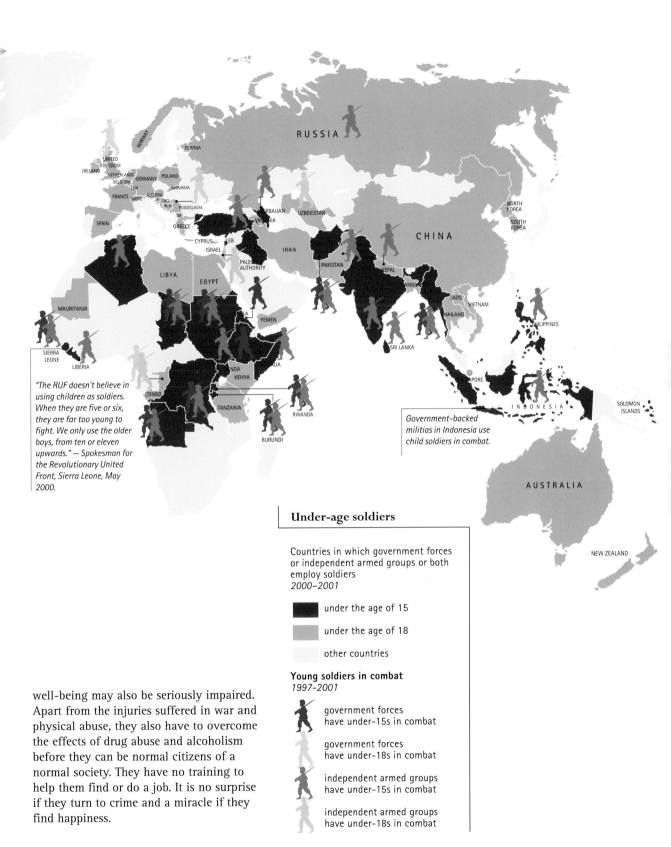

"The RUF doesn't believe in using children as soldiers. When they are five or six, they are far too young to fight. We only use the older boys, from ten or eleven upwards." — Spokesman for the Revolutionary United Front, Sierra Leone, May 2000.

Government-backed militias in Indonesia use child soldiers in combat.

## Under-age soldiers

Countries in which government forces or independent armed groups or both employ soldiers
*2000–2001*

- under the age of 15
- under the age of 18
- other countries

**Young soldiers in combat**
*1997-2001*

- government forces have under-15s in combat
- government forces have under-18s in combat
- independent armed groups have under-15s in combat
- independent armed groups have under-18s in combat

well-being may also be seriously impaired. Apart from the injuries suffered in war and physical abuse, they also have to overcome the effects of drug abuse and alcoholism before they can be normal citizens of a normal society. They have no training to help them find or do a job. It is no surprise if they turn to crime and a miracle if they find happiness.

# CHAPTER FOUR

# Europe

IN THE SECOND HALF OF THE TWENTIETH CENTURY, the number of people killed in wars in Europe was a little over half a million. In the first half of the century, the total was over 60 million.

In addition to the wars in Europe between 1900 and 1950, several European powers were engaged in colonial wars, trying to maintain a grip on their empires. Some of the most vicious episodes of Europe's colonial history —

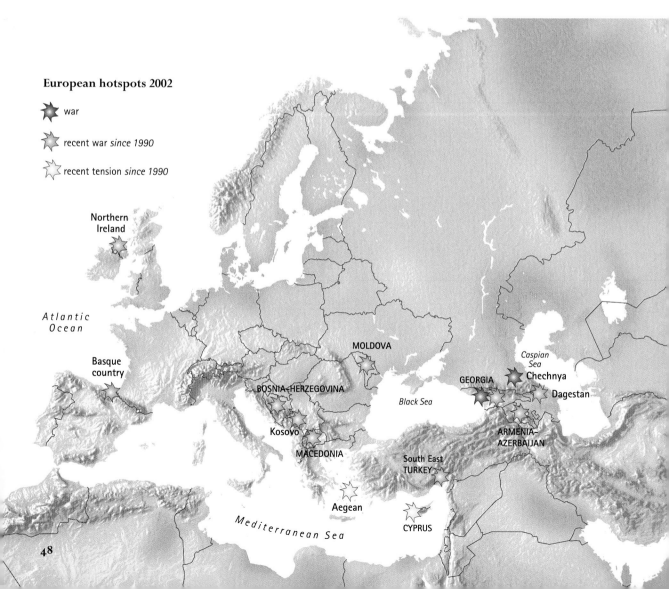

**European hotspots 2002**

⬟ war

⬟ recent war *since 1990*

☆ recent tension *since 1990*

Northern Ireland

*Atlantic Ocean*

Basque country

MOLDOVA

*Caspian Sea*

GEORGIA    Chechnya

BOSNIA-HERZEGOVINA

*Black Sea*    Dagestan

Kosovo

ARMENIA-AZERBAIJAN

MACEDONIA

South East TURKEY

Aegean

CYPRUS

*Mediterranean Sea*

Belgium in the Congo, Britain in Afghanistan and in India – happened during this period. The second half of the century was the era of European decolonization – again, with moments of great violence, such as France in Algeria and Portugal in Mozambique, but with an overall trend towards being less involved in armed conflict.

To most western Europeans it seemed that by about the 1980's the continent's time as a major originator of war, both overseas and at home, had come to an end. In the decades after World War Two, while Europe was heavily militarized as part of the East-West confrontation, there were few wars close to home. When East-West confrontation ended, it did so with little bloodshed. Despite continuing violence in Northern Ireland and the Basque region of Spain, there was a widespread sense that a new era of peace was dawning.

That is why the 1990s and the extreme violence of the break-up of Yugoslavia – and of some parts of the break-up of the USSR – came as such a shock. A western Europe that was becoming rather proud of itself and rather sure of its peaceful achievements proved to be unable to handle the violence in former Yugoslavia. It could not resolve it, suppress it, or control it, and could not persuade Balkan politicians to opt for compromise and peace.

Perhaps that was why western European leaders who tried to explain what was happening in southeastern Europe in the 1990s talked about it as if the people there were another species. They talked of hot-blooded tribes and ancient hatreds – though they also knew that when rival Balkan politicians met they were frequently friendly and sociable with each other.

What was happening in former Yugoslavia, as in the Caucasus, was a struggle for power, but one that was carried out without the rules of the democratic game that apply in western Europe. It was the absence of rules that was special, not the strength of national feeling, which is common in western Europe too, but is expressed in different ways.

A few years on from the worst of the carnage, western Europe is trying to bring southeastern Europe into its embrace. The prize it offers is a share in European modernity; the price is a complete change of style of political leadership. It is not just the specific people who must quit the political stage, but the political stage itself has to be rebuilt - along with comprehensive political and social reforms. In that sense, the European Union's recipe for peace is the European Union itself – boring, cooperative, businesslike, prosperous, inter-dependent, pragmatic – everything the Balkans and Caucasus have not been.

ONE HUNDRED YEARS OF WAR

# 18 | Northern Ireland

The first English attempt to conquer Ireland was in 1170. For the next 750 years there was intermittent and often brutal conflict until most of Ireland gained effective independence from an exhausted Britain just after World War One.

The partition of Ireland, and the creation of Northern Ireland, left unfinished business that was taken up in a small but nasty war starting 1970 and lasting another quarter century. But by the beginning of the 21st century, Ireland started to look as if it might be facing a period of peace.

To make peace, political leaders had to take risks. Republican leader Gerry Adams took the first risk by talking in Irish Republican circles about a political solution. Moderate nationalist leader John Hume took the next one by talking to Adams in 1993. British Prime Minister John Major and Irish

Taoiseach (Prime Minister) Albert Reynolds took the risk of jointly listening to them and publicly launched their peace initiative in December that year. In 1998 the new British and Irish leaders, Tony Blair and Bertie Aherne, staked all their political credibility on achieving a Peace Agreement, and Northern Ireland's Unionist leader David Trimble stood out ahead of much opinion in his own party and joined them.

With small setbacks and visible uncertainties on both sides of the political divide, the Northern Irish peace process has persisted. Several armed groups that were set up in the name of defending a community now devote themselves to brutally asserting their power within that community. Despite public fears and political complaints on each side about double-dealing on the other, too much has been gained from the peace process for rational politicians to abandon it.

From its foundation until the 1960s, Northern Ireland was ruled by a narrow local elite with the London government pursuing a determined policy of non-involvement. The basis for that sectarian

## The Death Toll

Number of people killed in the Northern Ireland conflict *1969-98*
Total deaths: 3,480
of which:
- 91% were male
- 53% were less than 30 years old
- 30% were Protestant
- 59% were killed by Republican paramilitary forces
- 28% were killed by Loyalist paramilitary forces
- 11% were killed by British security forces

## Population change in Northern Ireland

Catholics and Protestants as a proportion of the total population of Northern Ireland
*1951–2001*

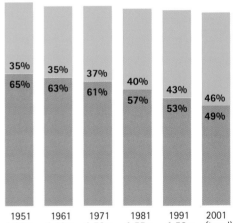

| | 1951 | 1961 | 1971 | 1981 | 1991 | 2001 *(trend)* |
|---|---|---|---|---|---|---|
| Protestant | 65% | 63% | 61% | 57% | 53% | 49% |
| Catholic | 35% | 35% | 37% | 40% | 43% | 46% |
| **Total population:** | **1.38m** | **1.43m** | **1.52m** | **1.55m** | **1.58m** | |

Death toll by year: 1969: 16; 1970: 26; 1971: 171; 1972: 479; 1973: 253; 1974: 294; 1975: 260; 1976: 295; 1977: 111; 1978: 81; 1979: 113; 1980: 80; 1981: 121; 1982: 110; 1983: 85; 1984: 69; 1985: 57; 1986: 61; 1987: 98; 1988: 104; 1989: 75; 1990: 81; 1991: 96; 1992: 89; 1993: 88; 1994: 64; 1995: 9; 1996: 18; 1997: 21; 1998: 55

statelet hardly exists today. The Protestant majority is vanishing. As the Catholic community edges towards the majority position, its leaders must decide how to respond to the temptation to retaliate for what the former majority inflicted on their parents.

If they succumb to that temptation, reverse discrimination will mean returning to protracted armed conflict, for there will be many leaders available who know how to feed resentment with fear.

## Catholic and Protestants by age groups in Northern Ireland

*1991*

Approximate total in each age group

1 million

42%

58%

0.4 million

53%

47%

Catholics

Protestants

0.2 million

31%

69%

| 0–15 years old | 16–64 (working age) | 65 and over |

## The island of Ireland

*late 1990s*
census and estimates

population total:
5.4 million

Catholics
4.15 million
77%

Protestants
1.1 million
20%

others
150,000
3%

## Northern Ireland

Catholics and Protestants as a proportion of the population, by local district
*1991 – latest census*

Catholic
70%–100%
50%–70%
30%–50%
0%–30%

Protestants
0%–30%
30%–50%
50%–70%
70%–100%

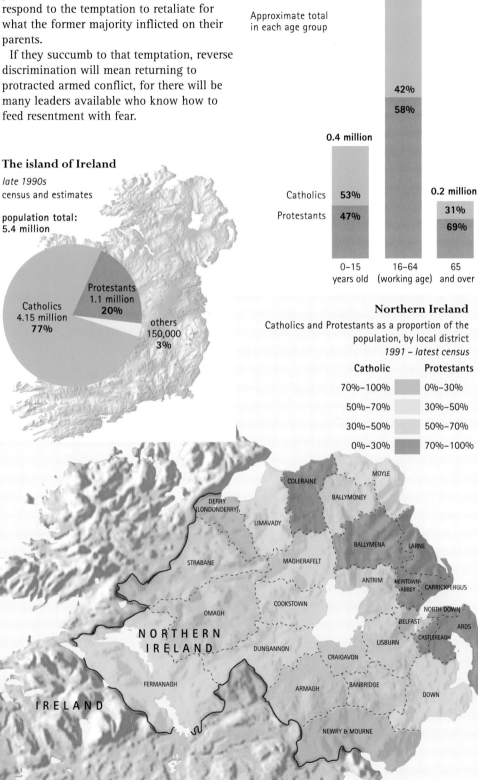

COLERAINE
MOYLE
DERRY (LONDONDERRY)
BALLYMONEY
LIMAVADY
BALLYMENA
LARNE
STRABANE
MAGHERAFELT
ANTRIM
NEWTOWN-ABBEY
CARRICKFERGUS
COOKSTOWN
NORTH DOWN
OMAGH
BELFAST
ARDS
NORTHERN IRELAND
DUNGANNON
LISBURN
CASTLEREAGH
CRAIGAVON
FERMANAGH
ARMAGH
BANBRIDGE
DOWN
IRELAND
NEWRY & MOURNE

1170 Norman invasion of Ireland from England.
1250 Normans control all Ireland.
1297 Uprisings confine Normans to small area around Dublin (the Pale).
1608 English and Scottish settlers imposed on Ulster (Northern Ireland).
1649 Cromwell ruler of England suppresses uprisings.
1690 King William III of England wins decisive victory at Battle of the Boyne, Northern Ireland.
1700 Irish Catholics deprived of property rights.

1790s 50,000 die in unsuccessful war of Irish independence led by Protestant lawyer Wolfe Tone.
1801 United Kingdom of Great Britain and Ireland established.
1840s–1860s Famines, uprisings, emigration.
1885–1914 Protestant businessmen, landowners and army block British government's attempts to grant Home Rule to Ireland.
1916 Easter Rising – insurrection put down by British.
1919–22 Irish Republican Army launches new war of independence.
1922–23 Civil war in Ireland over whether to accept British plan to partition Ireland.
1925 Partition agreed. Ireland independent, Northern Ireland remains in United Kingdom, with Protestant elite in control and Catholics' rights severely restricted.

1960s Civil rights campaign against anti-Catholic discrimination in Northern Ireland. Protestant backlash.
1969 Protestant march sparks violence in Derry. Riots. British army called in to restore order.
1970 Provisional IRA launches armed campaign.
1971 Internment without trial introduced. Violence escalates.

1993 New peace initiative by Gerry Adams (Leader of Sinn Fein) and John Hume (Leader of SDLP).
1994 IRA Ceasefire.
1998 Good Friday Peace Agreement signed. Referendums in Ireland and Northern Ireland give approval.
August: Bomb planted in Omagh by breakaway faction of the IRA, kills 29 people.
2001 IRA begins decommissioning weapons.
2002 First Irish Republican mayor of Belfast is elected.
2002 IRA apologises to families of "non-combatants" it killed during the fighting.

THE TROUBLES

# 19 The Break-up of Yugoslavia

Yugoslavia's disintegration began in 1991. In the following decade of warfare, over four million people – almost a quarter of the pre-war population – fled their homes and more than 150,000 were killed.

Yugoslavia was created by uniting nations with an already long history of fighting for political independence. Established as a kingdom in December 1918, it was broken up by the German occupation forces in World War Two, then reformed by the Communists under the leadership of Josip Broz Tito, who ruled until his death in 1980.

Tito maintained power through a mixture of repression, communist ideology and balanced concession to national sentiment. Following his death, there was a presidential council made up of the representatives of six republics and two provinces. Real power – except for the military and security services – steadily shifted from the Federal capital to the republics.

In 1987, Slobodan Milosevic used Serb nationalist sentiment about Kosovo to take power in Serbia and gain the upper hand in Yugoslavia as a whole. Milosevic removed the autonomy of the provinces of Kosovo and Vojvodina, and close allies took control in Montenegro.

First in Slovenia, then in Croatia, nationalist feelings rose in rivalry with Serbia. In 1991, both countries declared independence, as did Macedonia, followed by Bosnia-Herzegovina in 1992. There followed a short war in Slovenia, a six-month war in Croatia (July 1991-January 1992), and three and a half years of devastating war in Bosnia (1992-95), while Macedonia escaped war until 2001.

In Bosnia-Herzegovina, as well as war between the Bosnian government and the forces of the self-declared statelet of Republika Serbska, war broke out between Bosniak and Croat forces in central Bosnia in 1993. At peak the forces of Republika Serbska controlled almost 70 percent of the country. They used terror, including killings, concentration camps and mass rape, to expel virtually all Croats and Muslims (a national rather than religious group, though many do follow Islam).

UN forces arrived in Bosnia and Croatia in 1992. They held the ceasefire line in Croatia and tried to limit the destruction and suffering in Bosnia-Herzegovina. The UN Security Council changed the forces' mandate ten times in 20 months. Promising to set up "safe havens" it failed to back its decisions with sufficient forces.

In July 1995, the forces of Republika Serbska massacred over 7,000 Bosniak men in the UN "safe haven" of Srebrenica. In response, western policy changed. After Croatia regained Krajina, a combined offensive with Bosnia supported by US air power pushed Serb forces back. Under US pressure, a peace agreement was negotiated at Dayton Air Force Base, Ohio. Bosnia-Herzegovina remained one country, made up of two units, one of which was itself a federation of two units. Bosniaks, Croats and Serbs all had political power and the political leaders of each community kept veto power in the Federal parliament. The arrangement was cemented by deploying an international "Implementation Force" consisting initially of over 50,000 troops. It is administered by a "High Representative" of the international community. Reconstruction has been slow, reconciliation even slower. Some refugees have returned but much of Bosnia-Herzegovina remains ethnically divided. If foreign forces withdraw, war would probably return.

**Yugoslavia before the war**
Total population
1981 census: 22,427,585

The 1981 census of the Socialist Federal Republic of Yugoslavia provides the last reliable demographic picture of ex-Yugoslavia. It recognised **six nations**, *ten nationalities* and several other groups including Yugoslavs.

Others 1.5%
(including *Slovaks, Romanians, Ruthenians, Bulgarians, Turks, Czechs, Italians* and other groups)

Hungarians 1.9%
Montenegrins 2.6%
*Roma* 3.7%
Yugoslavs 5.4%
Macedonians 5.7%
*Albanians* 7.7%
Slovenes 7.8%
Muslims 8.7%
Croats 19.7%
Serbs 36.3%

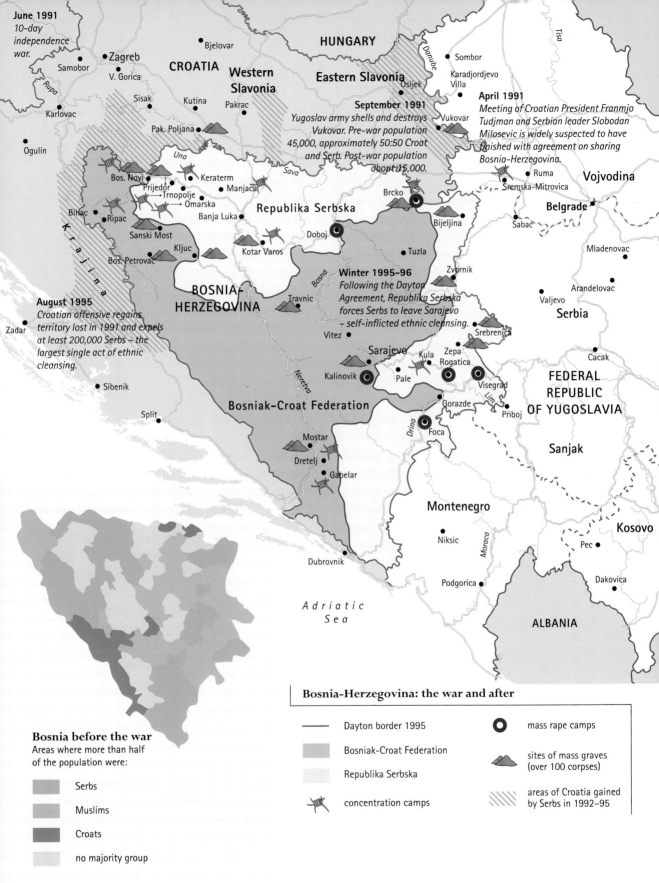

**June 1991**
*10-day independence war.*

September 1991
*Yugoslav army shells and destroys Vukovar. Pre-war population 45,000, approximately 50:50 Croat and Serb. Post-war population about 15,000.*

**April 1991**
*Meeting of Croatian President Franmjo Tudjman and Serbian leader Slobodan Milosevic is widely suspected to have finished with agreement on sharing Bosnia-Herzegovina.*

HUNGARY

CROATIA  Western Slavonia  Eastern Slavonia

Vojvodina

Belgrade

Republika Serbska

Bosniak-Croat Federation

BOSNIA-HERZEGOVINA

**Winter 1995-96**
*Following the Dayton Agreement, Republika Serbska forces Serbs to leave Sarajevo – self-inflicted ethnic cleansing.*

**August 1995**
*Croatian offensive regains territory lost in 1991 and expels at least 200,000 Serbs – the largest single act of ethnic cleansing.*

Serbia

FEDERAL REPUBLIC OF YUGOSLAVIA

Sanjak

Montenegro

Kosovo

*Adriatic Sea*

ALBANIA

**Bosnia before the war**
Areas where more than half of the population were:

Serbs

Muslims

Croats

no majority group

**Bosnia-Herzegovina: the war and after**

—————  Dayton border 1995

Bosniak-Croat Federation

Republika Serbska

concentration camps

mass rape camps

sites of mass graves (over 100 corpses)

areas of Croatia gained by Serbs in 1992–95

53

# 20 Kosovo and the War on Yugoslavia

Slobodan Milosevic rose to supreme power in Serbia by exploiting national sentiment. In the fall-out, Yugoslavia broke up and Serbia suffered economic disaster, military defeat and territorial loss.

Under Yugoslavia's 1974 constitution, Kosovo was an autonomous province within Serbia. After demonstrations in 1981 when demands were voiced for more autonomy, a Serb backlash began, slowly at first, gathering pace only when a rising Communist politician picked up the theme in 1987.

Milosevic used nationalism to cement his position in Serbia and to bid for further power in Yugoslavia. The removal of autonomy first from Vojvodina and then Kosovo were part of the process.

In 1991 Kosovars voted for an independent republic and withdrew from official politics. Milosevic's men stole the votes that Albanians did not cast in elections. When democratic Serbian opposition to Milosevic was strong in 1991 and again in 1996, there was no attempt to make common cause with Kosovars.

Kosovo first sought independence non-violently, expecting support from the international community. The November 1995 Dayton Agreement ending the war in Bosnia-Herzegovina ignored Kosovo. The Kosovo Liberation Army (KLA) made its first

September 1991
Kosovo deputies declare independent Republic of Kosovo.

Racak
January 1999
40 Albanians shot.

Gracanica
Serb enclave, high security village protected by international troops.

## Kosovo

↖ main routes taken by Kosovar refugees *1999*

///// refugee areas *1999*

▨ main areas where Serbs remain in Kosovo

public appearance in mid-1996, eight months later.

War began in February 1998. During the summer, some 250,000 Kosovars were forced from their homes. To end the violence, NATO threatened bombing. In October Milosevic agreed to a ceasefire. Over the winter, both the Serbian para-military police and the KLA continued their activity.

In the southern Kosovo village of Racak in January 1999, a Serbian police attack left 40 dead. Though the forensic evidence was inconclusive, official international observers treated the incident as a massacre of innocent civilians. It galvanized western public opinion.

The major powers summoned Serbian and Kosovar leaders to France and proposed increased autonomy for Kosovo with foreign military forces for security, with a future referendum on independence. Eventually the Kosovars accepted but the Serbs refused.

On 23 March 1999, bombing started. The US expected a short campaign. It lasted for 78 days. Within a few hours of the first bombs, the first Albanian village was emptied of inhabitants by the military, police and Serb volunteers. Nearly a million Albanians fled Kosovo.

In the UN Security Council, Russia and China would have vetoed the bombing in the UN Security Council. The west therefore never put the matter to the vote. The bombing campaign therefore contravened the terms of the UN Charter.

The deal that ended the bombing was nonetheless endorsed by the UN Security Council. It left Kosovo as part of Serbia with a considerable though undefined degree of autonomy (a constitutional framework was only drawn up two years later). NATO-led forces went in and the Serb and Yugoslav police and military pulled out. The UN in Kosovo administers the area. As international forces entered and Albanian refugees returned, over 100,000 Serbs left, some forced out, others leaving in fear of retribution.

While some public support rallied to Milosevic in Serbia, most blamed him for leading Serbia into a disastrous war. The normally divided democratic opposition managed to unite for the presidential election in September 2000. Vojislav Kostunica won and even Milosevic's team of experienced vote-riggers could do nothing. Faced by huge demonstrations in Belgrade, with tacit support from the army and police, Milosevic stepped down. In 2001 he was arrested and taken to the Hague to face trial for war crimes in Kosovo. Crimes in Bosnia and Croatia were later added to the charge sheet.

The new governments of Serbia and of Yugoslavia face a long and difficult task in overcoming the political, economic and social damage inflicted by 13 years of rule by Slobodan Milosevic.

## The Preshevo Valley

*In the Kumanovo agreement in June 1999, Serb and Yugoslav forces were excluded from the Preshevo Valley region of southern Serbia. To help undermine Milosevic, the USA supported the new Liberation Army of Preshevo, Medveda and Bujanovac, named after the three main towns in the region, and turned a blind but knowing eye as arms supplies were ferried over the border. Serious fighting broke out in late 2000, after Milosevic was ousted. Now NATO and Belgrade co-operated in keeping things under control. In May 2001, a peace agreement was signed promising economic development in the region, the Yugoslav army was allowed back into what had been an exclusion zone, and Preshevo Valley waited for economic investment.*

**RISE AND FALL OF A DICTATOR**

**Slobodan Milosevic**

**1941** Born.

**1962** Father commits suicide.

**1972** Mother commits suicide.

**1986** Becomes head of Serbian Communist Party (1990: changes name to Socialist Party of Serbia).

**1987** Supports Serb nationalists against Kosovo police, launches final rise to the top.

**1988** Manoeuvres allies into power in Vojvodina and Montenegro.

**1989** President of Serbia; forcibly revokes Kosovo's autonomy.

**1991** Mass demonstrations against Milosevic in Belgrade violently suppressed.

**1995** Signs Dayton Agreement to end war in Bosnia-Herzegovina on behalf of Bosnian Serbs.

**1996–97** Mass demonstrations in Belgrade against Milosevic's electoral fraud in Serbian local elections.

**1997** President of Federal Republic of Yugoslavia.

**1998** Agrees ceasefire in Kosovo.

**1999** Rejects international ultimatum to withdraw Serbian and Yugoslav forces from Kosovo.

**2000**
22 September: Loses Federal presidential elections 23 September, claims victory,
5 October: Ousted by mass demonstrations and army pressure.

**2001** Arrested and transferred to the Hague to face trial for crimes against humanity in Kosovo at the International Criminal Tribunal for Former Yugoslavia.

# 21 | Ex-Yugoslavia and the Future

In March 2002, the remaining two republics of Yugoslavia agreed to consign that name to the past. They agreed a new name – simply Serbia and Montenegro – and a new constitution for a provisional three-year period.

Of the components of what was the Socialist Federal Republic of Yugoslavia from 1945 until 1992, only Slovenia and Croatia, the first to leave, now have a clear and stable constitutional framework. For the rest, the basis on which politics happens – which country you are part of, who has what rights in it, and how government is chosen – could change radically in the coming years. Greater constitutional stability is one requirement if stable peace is to be built.

A second requirement is that the local economies have to be put in working order. War, sanctions and widespread corruption have taken a heavy toll of productivity and prosperity. A UN report on Kosovo in 2002, three years after international forces went in, found that half the population lived in poverty and one-eighth, or 12 percent, in extreme poverty. As in Bosnia-Herzegovina, the best jobs are found by working for international organizations, which means that many of the best trained people are not available for local businesses that might attract investment and be the motor for economic growth.

Corruption and criminality are widespread, reaching to the top of the political establishment throughout the region. A major drive against corruption is a third requirement for stable peace.

Until these requirements are met, international assistance is required. Outside help cannot solve the underlying problems, but it can hold them in check until local solutions emerge.

**The Hague: International Criminal Tribunal for the former Yugoslavia**
*Status July 2002*

*Total held in The Hague
as of July 2002:
47 – plus 9 temporarily
released pending trial*

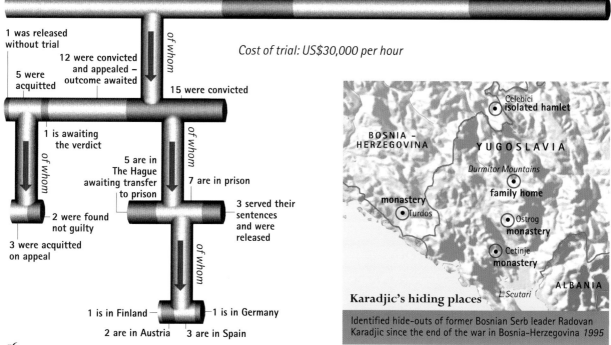

**93 individuals have been publicly indicted, of whom:**

**34 have been tried**    **11 are on trial**    **27 are going through pre-trial proceedings**    **21 are at large**

1 was released without trial

*of whom*

5 were acquitted

12 were convicted and appealed – outcome awaited

15 were convicted

*Cost of trial: US$30,000 per hour*

1 is awaiting the verdict

*of whom*

5 are in The Hague awaiting transfer to prison

7 are in prison

*of whom*

2 were found not guilty

3 served their sentences and were released

3 were acquitted on appeal

*of whom*

1 is in Finland — 1 is in Germany
2 are in Austria   3 are in Spain

**Karadjic's hiding places**

Celebici
isolated hamlet

BOSNIA - HERZEGOVINA

YUGOSLAVIA

Durmitor Mountains
family home

monastery
Turdos

Ostrog
monastery

Cetinje
monastery

L. Scutari

ALBANIA

Identified hide-outs of former Bosnian Serb leader Radovan Karadjic since the end of the war in Bosnia-Herzegovina *1995*

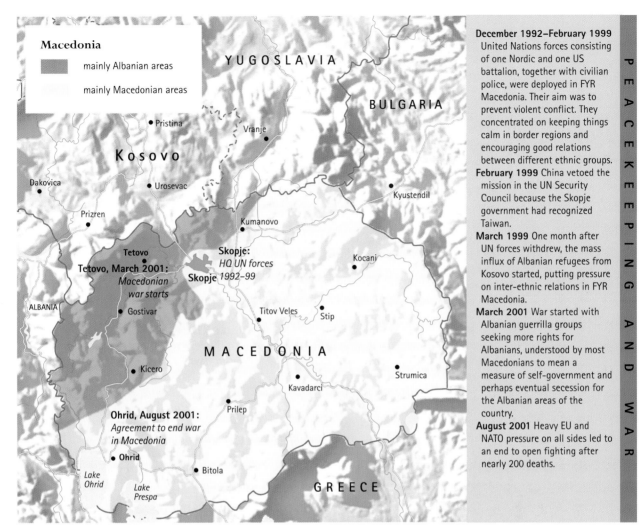

**Macedonia**

mainly Albanian areas

mainly Macedonian areas

YUGOSLAVIA

BULGARIA

KOSOVO

• Pristina

Vranje

Dakovica

• Urosevac

• Kyustendil

Prizren

Kumanovo

Tetovo

Kocani

**Tetovo, March 2001:**
*Macedonian war starts*

**Skopje:**
*HQ UN forces*
Skopje *1992–99*

ALBANIA

• Gostivar

Titov Veles

• Stip

MACEDONIA

• Kicero

Strumica

Kavadarci

**Ohrid, August 2001:**
*Agreement to end war in Macedonia*

Prilep

• Ohrid

• Bitola

*Lake Ohrid*

*Lake Prespa*

GREECE

**December 1992–February 1999**
United Nations forces consisting of one Nordic and one US battalion, together with civilian police, were deployed in FYR Macedonia. Their aim was to prevent violent conflict. They concentrated on keeping things calm in border regions and encouraging good relations between different ethnic groups.

**February 1999** China vetoed the mission in the UN Security Council because the Skopje government had recognized Taiwan.

**March 1999** One month after UN forces withdrew, the mass influx of Albanian refugees from Kosovo started, putting pressure on inter-ethnic relations in FYR Macedonia.

**March 2001** War started with Albanian guerrilla groups seeking more rights for Albanians, understood by most Macedonians to mean a measure of self-government and perhaps eventual secession for the Albanian areas of the country.

**August 2001** Heavy EU and NATO pressure on all sides led to an end to open fighting after nearly 200 deaths.

SLOVENIA

CROATIA

Vojvodina

ROMANIA

### Bosnia-Herzegovina

A union of two entities – Republika Srpska and the Federation (itself made up of two units), will it be one, two, or three states? The international community wants one state – many Bosnian Serb and Bosnian Croatian politicians are not so sure.

BOSNIA-HERZEGOVINA

Serbia

### Serbia and Montenegro

March 2002: three year arrangement for loose union, renamed from Federal Republic of Yugoslavia. The agreement came as a result of heavy pressure from the EU, which was determined to stop Montenegrin independence. Future uncertain.

Montenegro

Kosovo

### Macedonia

Constitutional amendments to encourage greater Albanian participation in the state, agreed as part of the August 2001 peace deal, are regarded as not enough by many Albanians and far too much by many Macedonians.

MACEDONIA

### Kosovo

Constitutional framework promulgated 2001 by UN Mission. Whether the province will ultimately remain part of Serbia is not yet decided. Strong opposing views are held by Albanians and Serbs. The international community seems uncertain.

ITALY

ALBANIA

GREECE

**Constitutional uncertainty**

# 22 | The Caucasus

The Caucasus is a region of 51 languages where state borders and nations do not match. In the late 1980s, the Armenian and Georgian drive for independence contributed to the crisis that caused the USSR to break up in 1991. But the desire for independence was also strong in areas within the post-Soviet states. New leaders in Chechnya sought freedom from Russia, Abkhazia from Georgia, and divided people such as the Ossetians and Lezghins looked for political unity.

Dreams of prosperity and freedom soured as conflicts escalated. Some of the key political leaders had little experience, not much sense of responsibility and no democratic constraints. Inevitably it was the ordinary people who suffered. The first half of the 1990s was the worst period – so bad that migration reduced Armenia's population by 25 to 30 percent.

Firm rule in Georgia and Azerbaijan by veteran Soviet politicians, Russia's military presence and the watchful eye of international observers have suppressed most of the conflicts – but not solved them.

Conflict between Russia and Chechnya has not even been suppressed. Russia lost the first war in 1994-96, and has been bogged down since launching a new war in 1999. Russia controls the ghost capital of Grozny, but Russian troops are attacked every day by Chechen guerrillas whom they outnumber almost 20 to 1. Russian forces respond to attacks by sweeps through villages, giving the underpaid and poorly motivated Russian soldiers a chance to rob and brutalize the villagers. In October 2002, Chechen guerrillas brought the war to Moscow, taking over a packed theatre and holding the audience hostage. The Russian rescue mission went horribly wrong, killing 100 of the hostages with a narcotic gas. Peace is not yet in sight.

Outside interest in the region is not only due to war, instability and their consequences. Caspian oil may be five percent of world oil output by 2020 – significant enough for US, Russian and Iranian interests to clash over the best route for a new pipeline. In the Caucasus, Azerbaijan will benefit most.

## World War Two

*Josef Stalin accused whole nations of collaborating with Germany during World War Two. In February 1944, Soviet security forces rounded up all Chechens (pop. 400,000) and Ingush (pop. 100,000) and 100,000 others from the north Caucasus and deported them in cattle trucks to central Asia. Thousands died on the journey. Return was not allowed until 1957.*

## Language groups in the Caucasus

- **Altaic (or Turkic)** language group – 6 languages including Azerbaijani

**Caucasian language group**

- **North West Caucasian** sub-group – 3 languages including Abkhaz
- **Nakh (or Vaynakh)** sub-group – 3 languages including Chechen and Ingush
- **Dagestani** – 28 languages including Lezgi
- **Kartvelian** – 3 languages including Georgian and Mingrelian

**Indo-European language group**

- **Iranian** sub-group – 4 languages including Kurdish and Ossetian
- **Slavic** sub-group – 2 languages (Russian and Ukrainian)
- **Armenian**
- **Greek**

RUSSIA
KARACHAI-CHERKESSIA
Mozdok
KABARDINO-BALKARIA
CHECHNYA
Black Sea
INGUSHETIA
ABKHAZIA
Sukhumi
NORTH OSSETIA
Grozny
Caspian Sea
Vladikavkaz
SOUTH OSSETIA
DAGESTAN
Tskhinval
Batumi
GEORGIA
Tbilisi
ADJARIA
TURKEY
ARMENIA
AZERBAIJAN
Baku
Yerevan
NAGORNO KARABAKH
NAKHICHEVAN
IRAN

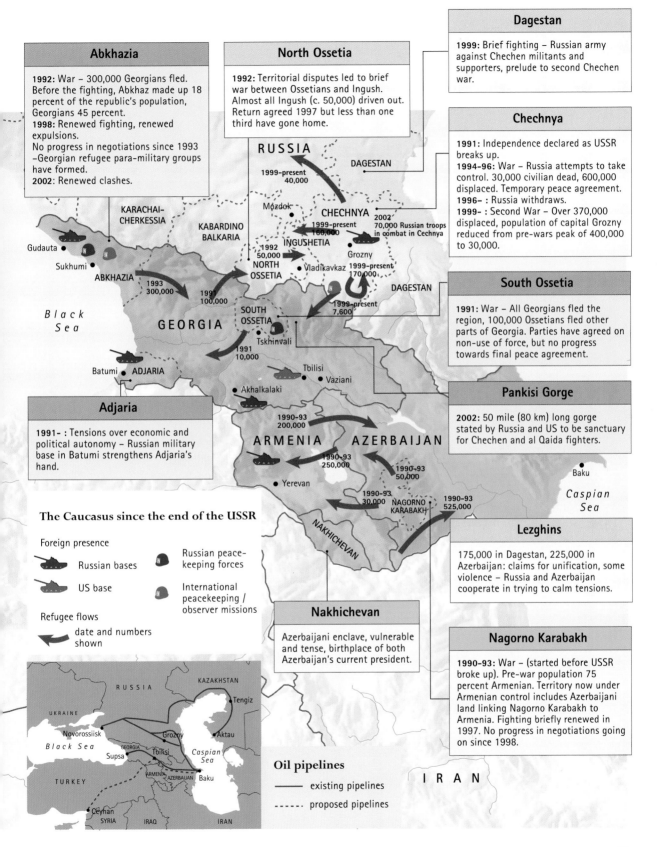

## Abkhazia

**1992:** War – 300,000 Georgians fled. Before the fighting, Abkhaz made up 18 percent of the republic's population, Georgians 45 percent.
**1998:** Renewed fighting, renewed expulsions.
No progress in negotiations since 1993 –Georgian refugee para-military groups have formed.
**2002:** Renewed clashes.

## North Ossetia

**1992:** Territorial disputes led to brief war between Ossetians and Ingush. Almost all Ingush (c. 50,000) driven out. Return agreed 1997 but less than one third have gone home.

## Dagestan

**1999:** Brief fighting – Russian army against Chechen militants and supporters, prelude to second Chechen war.

## Chechnya

**1991:** Independence declared as USSR breaks up.
**1994-96:** War – Russia attempts to take control. 30,000 civilian dead, 600,000 displaced. Temporary peace agreement.
**1996–ؘ :** Russia withdraws.
**1999–ؘ :** Second War – Over 370,000 displaced, population of capital Grozny reduced from pre-wars peak of 400,000 to 30,000.

## South Ossetia

**1991:** War – All Georgians fled the region, 100,000 Ossetians fled other parts of Georgia. Parties have agreed on non-use of force, but no progress towards final peace agreement.

## Pankisi Gorge

**2002:** 50 mile (80 km) long gorge stated by Russia and US to be sanctuary for Chechen and al Qaida fighters.

## Adjaria

**1991– :** Tensions over economic and political autonomy – Russian military base in Batumi strengthens Adjaria's hand.

## Lezghins

175,000 in Dagestan, 225,000 in Azerbaijan: claims for unification, some violence – Russia and Azerbaijan cooperate in trying to calm tensions.

## Nakhichevan

Azerbaijani enclave, vulnerable and tense, birthplace of both Azerbaijan's current president.

## Nagorno Karabakh

**1990-93:** War – (started before USSR broke up). Pre-war population 75 percent Armenian. Territory now under Armenian control includes Azerbaijani land linking Nagorno Karabakh to Armenia. Fighting briefly renewed in 1997. No progress in negotiations going on since 1998.

### The Caucasus since the end of the USSR

Foreign presence

Russian bases

US base

Russian peace-keeping forces

International peacekeeping / observer missions

Refugee flows

date and numbers shown

Oil pipelines

—— existing pipelines

----- proposed pipelines

*Map labels:* RUSSIA, KARACHAI-CHERKESSIA, KABARDINO BALKARIA, DAGESTAN, Mozdok, CHECHNYA, INGUSHETIA, Grozny, Vladikavkaz, NORTH OSSETIA, DAGESTAN, Gudauta, Sukhumi, ABKHAZIA, 1993 300,000, 1991 100,000, Black Sea, GEORGIA, SOUTH OSSETIA, Tskhinvali, 1991 10,000, Batumi, ADJARIA, Akhalkalaki, Tbilisi, Vaziani, 1990-93 200,000, ARMENIA, AZERBAIJAN, 1990-93 250,000, 1990-93 50,000, Yerevan, 1990-93 30,000, NAGORNO KARABAKH, 1990-93 525,000, Baku, Caspian Sea, NAKHICHEVAN, IRAN, 1999-present 40,000, 1999-present 160,000, 1992 50,000, 1999-present 170,000, 1999-present 7,600, 2002 70,000 Russian troops in combat in Cechnya

*Inset map labels:* RUSSIA, KAZAKHSTAN, UKRAINE, Tengiz, Novorossiisk, Grozny, Aktau, Black Sea, GEORGIA, Supsa, Tbilisi, Caspian Sea, ARMENIA, AZERBAIJAN, Baku, TURKEY, Ceyhan, SYRIA, IRAQ, IRAN

# CHAPTER FIVE

# Middle East and North Africa

## UN Human Development Index
*2002*

Israel 22
*highest in region*

Bahrain 39

Kuwait 45, UAE 46

Qatar 51

Libya 64

Saudi Arabia 71

Lebanon 75
Oman 78

Tunisia 97, Iran 98, Jordan 99

Algeria 106
Syria 108

Egypt 115

Morocco 123

Yemen 144
*lowest in region*

THE ARAB WORLD AND THE MIDDLE EAST are not synonymous, for the region includes non-Arab states, (Iran, Israel), and Arab states themselves are ethnically diverse. Nonetheless, understanding the Middle East necessitates understanding Arab dilemmas. Despite oil wealth in some parts of the Middle East and North Africa, much of it is poor. Despite a long tradition of higher education, adult literacy in the region is under 60 percent. Despite having so much in common with each other in language, religion and culture, the region's Arab states are divided and often at cross purposes with each other.

The Arab Middle East has had great difficulty working out a viable relationship with the west since, at the end of the 18th century, a European conquered Egypt. Napoleon Bonaparte's short-lived rule in Egypt was a shock to the Ottoman and Arab ruling elites in the Middle East, most of whom still viewed Europe as an impoverished, weak, backward and barbaric region – a view that had been well justified a century earlier. Now Europe had military superiority, greater wealth, better technology and more efficient leadership. By the end of the 19th century, most of North Africa was in European hands. When the Ottoman Empire collapsed at the end of World War One, Britain and France divided up much of the rest of the Middle East between them.

Beginning in the 19th century and throughout the 20th, Arab thinkers have debated

how to relate to Europe – to copy it, to shun it or to take those bits that seemed to fit Arab ways – but arrived at no obvious conclusion.

The discovery of oil and independence from the Europeans might have combined together to provide both the resources and the energy for a great Arab revival. But the central significance of oil in modern economies brought the greater power of the USA into the regional picture, and the problems within and between Arab countries proved too numerous and too hard to deal with. Even in the Gulf region with copious oil wealth, economic development was slow. Much of the new wealth has been spent on extravagances for the ruling families while the populations of both oil rich and non-oil Arab countries have gained little.

Beyond the social inequalities and economic inefficiencies, the political unity necessary to achieve something approaching parity with the West was lacking. There has been unity in only one thing – the loathing of what is understood in the Arab world as the Western imposition of the state of Israel on their region. Even that unity turned out to be strictly limited once Israel had repeatedly demonstrated its military capacities and internal unity when under fire, and the strength of its US support. Only in the 1970s when oil was used as an instrument of Arab diplomacy to isolate Israel did Arab leaders briefly show the unity and consistency of purpose needed to shake Western policy over the Middle East.

At the start of the 21st century, the dilemma of how to relate to the West – of how to balance continuity and modernity – remains unresolved. Extreme violence, to which a very small number of people have turned, has grabbed horrified Western attention. It sits at the extreme rejectionist end of the spectrum of choices about the relationship with the West. Most opinion leaders throughout the Middle East and North Africa have rejected it on moral grounds. A way forward has yet to emerge.

## Middle East and North African hotspots 2002

 war

 recent war
*since 1990*

 recent tension
*since 1990*

# 23 | The Kurds

The Kurdish people are united by geography, by history and by their name. Almost everything else divides them. They have never had a unified state.

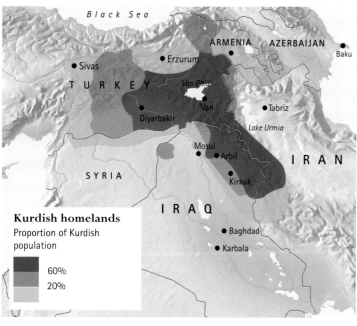

**Kurdish homelands**
Proportion of Kurdish population

60%
20%

**The State of Kurdistan**
Proposed by Treaty of Sèvres
*1920*

proposed state

to be given choice of joining after 1922

In the early 1990s, the uprising by Iraqi Kurds led to one and a half million people fleeing their homes, and to a wave of concern for their plight in Europe and North America. At the same time there was a long war against the Turkish state by Turkish Kurds. By the end of the millennium, the great powers had stabilized northern Iraq and the civil war in Turkey was all but over. The situation of the Kurds now received far less international attention, but in many respects they were not much better off than a decade earlier.

For centuries the people of the mountains of Kurdistan were beyond the reach of the empires that sought to control the region. Isolation bred a common sense of identity despite many differences of language and custom.

The last real chance for an autonomous and united Kurdistan came with the end of World War One. In the 1920 Treaty of Sèvres, the parcelling out of territory from the broken Ottoman Empire provided for a Kurdish nation state in a two stage process: part of Anatolian Kurdistan was to be recognised as the new state immediately, and part of Iraqi Kurdistan was to be given the choice of joining after 1922.

But at the same time, modern Turkey was being created out of the ruins of the Ottoman Empire. Turkey's new leader, the brilliant General Mustafa Kemal Atatürk refused to cede any land to the proposed Kurdish state, even though Kurdish troops had helped Atatürk to power.

Britain and France, both satisfied with their own territorial gains in the region, were wary of disturbing a fragile peace, were tired of war and faced pressing problems elsewhere in their imperial domains. They backed down and in 1923 a new treaty was agreed. With that, united Kurdistan was lost. In 1925, a Kurdish uprising in Turkey was crushed, leaving 250,000 dead.

Kurdish politics often show bitter internal divisions. Since the 1920s, Kurds have fought for independence from Iraq in a succession of uprisings. Every uprising until the 1980s met armed opposition from rival Kurdish factions as well as the Baghdad authorities. In the 1990s rival Kurdish groups in northern Iraq went to war with each other. Iraqi Kurdish forces have helped Turkish military campaigns inside northern Iraq against the armed group, the Turkish Kurdistan Workers Party, the PKK.

The PKK's war for autonomy for the largely Kurdish southeastern part of Turkey started in 1984. It was led by Abdullah Öçalan, who operated from headquarters in Syria. During the war large areas were depopulated by the Turkish army to deny local support to the PKK, who themselves systematically killed Kurds whom they accused of serving the Turkish state, such as school-teachers.

When Öçalan lost Syrian support in 1998, and with it that safe haven, he had to flee, seeking asylum in Italy. The Italian government refused to extradite Öçalan to Turkey because Turkey still had the death penalty. In January 1999, Öçalan vanished, to be found in Kenya where he was arrested the following month on his way from the Greek embassy to try to find another refuge. He was taken back to Turkey, tried and condemned, but not executed. Greek-Turkish relations suffered, but recovered in mid-1999 to move to their friendliest for many years. Meanwhile Öçalan called for a truce; in February 2000 the PKK announced an end to the war, which had cost 30,000 lives.

Despite occasional armed clashes, southeastern Turkey was more peaceful in 2002 than at any time in the preceding 20 years. Economic development still lags behind the rest of Turkey. The PKK has attempted to transform itself into a political party – the Congress for Freedom and Democracy in Kurdistan (KADEC) – which the Turkish government sees as a purely cosmetic change.

In northern Iraq, open warfare in the mid-1990s between the two main Kurdish groups – the Kurdistan Democratic Party (KDP) and the Patriotic Union of Kurdistan (PUK) – has been replaced by a tense stand-off and occasional assassinations, bombings and clashes. Under the control of these groups, and protected from Iraqi air power by the no-fly zone established in 1991 by Britain, France, Turkey and the USA, most of Iraqi Kurdistan is effectively autonomous. As the USA contemplated an attack on Iraq in 2002, plans were aired for creating a federal Iraq, with an Arab component in the south and Kurdish semi-independence in the north. Supporting Kurdish autonomy, however, was not to Turkey's taste.

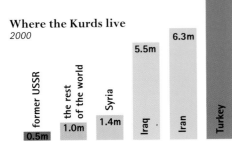

## Where the Kurds live
*2000*

| former USSR | the rest of the world | Syria | Iraq | Iran | Turkey |
|---|---|---|---|---|---|
| 0.5m | 1.0m | 1.4m | 5.5m | 6.3m | 15.5m |

## Control of Iraqi Kurdistan
*1998*

Kurdistan Democratic Party (KDP)

Patriotic Union of Kurdistan (PUK)

*"no fly zone" policed by France, Turkey, UK, USA established 1991*

# 24 | Israel and Palestine

In 1993 Israeli Prime Minister Yitzhak Rabin and PLO Chairman Yasser Arafat shook hands at the White House. It marked an opportunity for peace but became one of many failures.

Israel has fought five international wars and faced constant conflict including two major uprisings. The first war started the day after its foundation and brought expansion. Further wars followed in 1956, 1967, 1973 and 1982. Neither taken singly nor together have these wars produced peace and security for Israel.

Having been unable to prevent Israel's foundation, the Arab states in 1964 committed themselves to Israel's destruction and supported the establishment of the Palestine Liberation Organization. The 1967 war revealed their military weakness again and the weakness of their unity was shown in 1970 when Jordan, seeing the PLO as a threat, expelled it.

Disunity arose again after the 1973 war. Egyptian President Sadat opted for diplomacy to retrieve territory lost in 1967. He got the agreement he wanted, but was isolated in the Arab world, while Israel opened up a new front in Lebanon.

Neither arms nor diplomacy nor increasing oil prices to diminish western support for Israel produced peace or security for Palestinians.

A spontaneous Palestinian uprising against occupation and for independence – the *intifada* – started in late 1987, sparked by a random incident (a car accident). The Israeli answer to stones and Molotov cocktails was tear gas, rubber bullets, beatings, detentions, deportations, house demolitions, and shooting at demonstrators. The Israeli government termed this response an "iron fist" but it could not end the uprising, which endangered Israel's reputation rather than its existence.

**1918** Palestine under British mandate

**1947** Israel in UN partition plan

**1949** Israel including annexed territory

**1967 War** Israel and Occupied Territories

**1978** Israel withdraws from Sinai

## Imbalance of power
Israeli and Palestinian armed forces *2002*

**Israel**: Army 120,000 plus 400,000 ready reservists
3,930 main battle tanks
5,500 armoured personnel carriers
1,375 field artillery
200 multiple rocket launchers
6,500 mortars
446 combat aircraft
133 armed helicopters

### Palestine Authority
Paramilitary: 35,000 including police, intelligence services, customs etc
45 armoured personnel carriers
1 non-combat aircraft
4 helicopters

### Palestinian groups
1,000 in Hamas & Islamic Jihad
several hundred in other groups in Occupied Territories
several thousand based in Iraq, Syria, Lebanon

Both sides were in a "no win" situation and entered secret talks arranged by the Norwegian government.

The PLO had accepted the principle of recognizing Israel's sovereignty over 78 percent of historical Palestine in return for independence. The Oslo process deliberately left the most difficult issues for later and attempted to get a peace momentum underway. Arafat returned to the Occupied Territories, the Palestine Authority was set up, elections were held, and some land was returned to Palestinian control.

Corruption was rife in the Palestine Authority, Israel did nothing to help – and much to hinder – economic development in the Occupied Territories, and all around the violence continued. In early 1996, a senior Hamas official died when his cellphone exploded. Hamas blamed the Israeli security service and responded with suicide bombings. In the tense atmosphere, Benjamin Netanyahu, an opponent of the Oslo process, was elected Prime Minister of Israel. Though negotiations continued, progress ceased.

In July 2000, Israel made a territorial offer that was, in the government's view, as generous as possible, perhaps too generous for the Israeli public to approve. For the Palestinian negotiators, however, the offer was far short of acceptable. The last effort to negotiate ended in January 2001.

In September 2000, Ariel Sharon took a highly publicized walk in the area of Haram al Sharif/Temple Mount, revered by Jews as the site of the first and second temples and by Muslims as the place from which the Prophet Muhammed ascended to heaven. Palestinians saw Sharon's visit as deliberate provocation; it triggered the second *intifada*.

On both sides, the tactics of the second *intifada* were harder than the first, especially after Sharon's election as Israel's Prime Minister: suicide bombings and drive-by shootings by the Palestinians; rocket attacks, targeted killings and tank assaults by Israel. By mid-2002, these attacks had destroyed much of the PA's administrative infrastructure – its capacity to exert authority. Then Israel started to build a physical wall between itself and the West Bank. This will cut the societies off from each other, but determined individuals will find a way round it. There is no evidence that any of these tactics offer any gain in peace or security to any person living in the area of Israel, Gaza or the West Bank.

## Israel – Control of territory in 2001 before Israeli reoccupation

- Israel
- areas under full Palestinian control
- areas under Palestinian administration with Israeli security control
- occupied areas under full Israeli control

**1982** Israel invades Lebanon. The PLO is forced to leave Beirut for Tunis.

**1987** *Intifada*: Palestinian uprising launched 8 December against Israeli occupation.

**1988** PLO recognises Israel's sovereignty over its own territory – 78% of historical Palestine – and declares independence for a state of Palestine.

**1990** As USSR breaks up, Russian migration to Israel accelerates: 187,000 immigrants in one year – Israel's highest ever annual figure.

**1991** PLO support for Iraq in Gulf War leads to expulsion of Palestinians from Kuwait. 370,000 return to Occupied Territories and Jordan.

**1993** Oslo process: secret talks lead to PLO and Israel signing the Declaration of Principles for peace.

**1994** Yasser Arafat returns to Occupied Territories. Israel and Jordan sign peace agreement. Nobel Peace Prize awarded to Arafat, Israeli Premier Yitzak Rabin and Foreign Minister Shimon Peres. Israeli settler, Baruch Goldstein, kills 29 Palestinian worshippers in Hebron mosque.

**1995** Further Israeli-PLO peace agreement. Rabin assassinated by Israeli extremist.

**1996** Arafat elected President of Palestine Authority. Israeli election won by Benjamin Netanyahu. New settlements constructed in Occupied Territories.

**1998** Wye River Memorandum signed by Arafat and Netanyahu, agreeing to implement agreements made earlier. Never implemented.

**2000** Israel withdraws from Southern Lebanon.
July: Israel and PLO fail to reach further agreement.
September: Second *Intifada*.

**2001** Ariel Sharon elected Prime Minister.

**2002** Israel reoccupies the West Bank.

# 25 Israelis and Palestinians

## Water
Average daily consumption

Palestinians: 60 liters

Israelis: 350 liters

Upon occupying the West Bank in 1967 Israel declared all water resources to be its property and instituted a strict system of licensing the construction of new wells and pipes. Since 1982, increased Israeli use has dried up Palestinian wells. Israel is slow to approve new water projects for Palestinian use, controls how much water can be used by Palestinians and does not hide that more water goes to the Jewish settlements in the Occupied Territories than to the ordinary Palestinian residents.

In the first two years of the second *intifada*, over 1,600 Palestinians and 550 Israelis were killed. Israelis lived in constant fear of new suicide attacks in public places – restaurants, shops, town centres. Palestinians have faced nights of shelling, week long curfews, endless checkpoints and house searches. Even apart from the impact of fear, ordinary life became harder. Israelis faced higher taxes, while the number living below the poverty line increased to 20 percent, and men of military age were called up to the army. Palestinians faced severe shortages of food, water and medicines. It was estimated that two million Palestinians received their food from humanitarian organizations.

About one million Palestinians live in Israel as citizens of the country. They can vote but have limited property rights. About 175,000 have had their property confiscated. They live in enclaves with an unemployment rate 66 percent higher than the Israeli average. When the new *intifada* started in the Occupied Territories, there was some unrest in the Palestinian areas of Israel. Israeli authorities stopped it at the cost of 13 Palestinian deaths and many injuries. On current trends, the Palestinian percentage of the population of Israel will more than double in the next 50 years to about 30 percent.

Outside Israel proper, Palestinians are the largest group of refugees in the world today. The first wave of flight came with the foundation of Israel in 1948 when over 80 percent of Palestinians left. The second wave came in 1967 as the West Bank and Gaza were conquered by Israel. The Palestinian refugee population of 3.8 million is increasing by about 3 percent a year.

Israel rejects the right of "return" for the refugees and displaced persons. They want to solve the problem by resettlement in Arab countries, international efforts to improve the refugees' living conditions and restricted readmission. The PLO insists on the absolute right of return for all Palestinian refugees of 1948.

## Fenced off

⊙    Palestinian towns

△    Israeli settlements

——   security fence

**2002:** Israel started construction of a security fence dividing the Occupied Territory of the West Bank from Israel proper.

## The population pendulum
Israel and the Occupied Territories

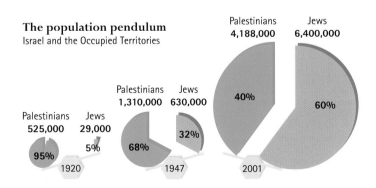

| | |
|---|---|
| Palestinians 525,000 | Jews 29,000 |
| 95% | 5% |
| 1920 | |

| | |
|---|---|
| Palestinians 1,310,000 | Jews 630,000 |
| 68% | 32% |
| 1947 | |

| | |
|---|---|
| Palestinians 4,188,000 | Jews 6,400,000 |
| 40% | 60% |
| 2001 | |

Umm el Fahm · Salem · Barta'a · Jenin · Naziat Issa · Baka as-Sharqiyeh · Tulkarem · Kalkilya · Nablus · West Bank · ISRAEL · Ramallah · Jericho · Jerusalem · JORDAN · Jordan · Dead Sea

## Refugees – and their refuges

Location of Palestinian refugees and displaced people
*2001*

up to 10,000

10,000 – 100,000

100,000 – 500,000

500,000 – one million

over one million

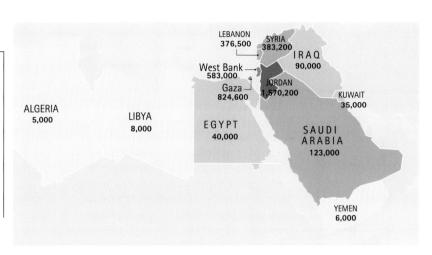

LEBANON
**376,500**

SYRIA
**383,200**

IRAQ
**90,000**

West Bank
**583,000**

JORDAN
**1,570,200**

Gaza
**824,600**

KUWAIT
**35,000**

ALGERIA
**5,000**

LIBYA
**8,000**

EGYPT
**40,000**

SAUDI
ARABIA
**123,000**

YEMEN
**6,000**

## Gaza
People per square km in settlements and other Israeli-controlled areas

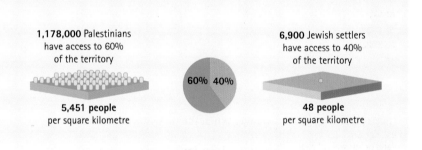

**1,178,000** Palestinians have access to 60% of the territory

**5,451 people**
per square kilometre

60% 40%

**6,900** Jewish settlers have access to 40% of the territory

**48 people**
per square kilometre

## Settlers in the Occupied Territories
total settler population

2001–02: 34 new settlements established in 12 months

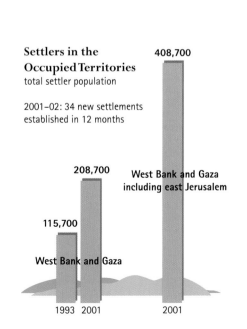

**408,700**

**208,700**

West Bank and Gaza including east Jerusalem

**115,700**

West Bank and Gaza

1993  2001

2001

Kochav Ya'acov

Ma'ale Mikhmas

Givat Ze'et

Sha'ar Binyamin

Ataro

Adam

**1980**: Declares Jerusalem to be capital of Israel

Neve Ya'acov

**West Bank**

Ramot

Pisgat Ze'et

Almon

Ramat Shu'fat

WEST  EAST

ISRAEL

Jerusalem
Old City

**1967**: Israel takes over east Jerusalem

Ma'ale Adumim

**1948**: Israel takes over west Jerusalem

Kedar

Talpiot

## Greater Jerusalem

Gilo

Har Gilo

Har Homa

existing and projected Israeli areas in and around east Jerusalem

- - - - occupied east Jerusalem

There are ambitious plans for urban development to the east of Jerusalem. These will have the effect of surrounding Palestinian areas of East Jerusalem with Israeli areas.

Since the start of the first *intifada* the Israeli authorities have ordered the demolition at least 2,450 houses in the Occupied Territories leaving over 16,000 Palestinians homeless.

# 26 North Africa

Having come under European control in the 19th and early 20th centuries, the countries of North Africa successfully gained independence in the 1950s. Like many other former parts of the European empires, however, the achievement of independence was by no means the solution to every problem facing the countries and their people. Other challenges of development have not been met so successfully, such as economic growth, a reasonable degree of individual prosperity, personal freedoms, increasing opportunities for education, stable and democratic government.

## Algeria

**1962** Independence from France after 8-year war that killed 500,000 people.

**1986** Rising inflation and unemployment, made worse by the collapse of oil and gas prices, led to a wave of strikes and violent demonstrations.

**1989** Islamic Salvation Front (FIS) was founded, winning 55 percent of the vote in local elections the following year.

**1991** FIS called a general strike to block Government plans to change the electoral system. FIS won the first round of national elections. Fighting started, a state of emergency was declared.

**1992** Military pressure forced a change of government and suspension of elections. FIS was banned, the Armed Islamic Group (GIA) emerged, and open war began.

**1995** Though its strength was badly damaged by the GIA, the army rejected a peace initiative brokered by mediators from the Rome-based Sant' Egidio Community, reorganised itself and launched "total war". By 1997 some of the armed opposition was ready to declare a ceasefire but the GIA fought on. Massacres of civilians started to be a feature of the war.

**1999** Abdelaziz Bouteflikka elected President with policy of "civil concord" offering amnesty to opposition fighters. Violence decreased.

**2000** Violence escalated again after the amnesty deadline passed. Hopes of peace declined and in parliamentary elections in 2002 over 50 percent of registered voters abstained.

## Morocco

**1956** Independence from France as a monarchy, ruled by King Hassan from 1961.

**1975** To reinforce his claim to Western (then Spanish) Sahara, despite the UN finding that the Saharawis wanted independence, Hassan organized 200,000 unarmed volunteers to march across the border. Avoiding confrontation, Spain quit the territory (last troops left in 1976). Armed independence struggle was launched by the Popular Front for the Liberation of Saguia el Hamra and Rio de Oro (Polisario), actively supported by Algeria and later by Libya.

**late 1980s** Polisario was out-powered in the war and out-manoeuvred in diplomacy as improving relations between Morocco and Algeria led the latter to do less for Polisario.

**1991** A UN resolution called for a referendum to decide whether Western Sahara should be independent or annexed to Morocco. Fighting ended, but disputes followed about who had the right to vote. A decade later, the referendum had not been held.

**1999** King Hassan died, succeeded by his son Mohammed VI.

**2002** Morocco and Spain in military confrontation over Parsley Island, uninhabited, 200 metres from Moroccan coast. Rest of world much amused.

5.4
MOROCCO

1975–91 war against independence for Western Sahara

6.5
ALGERIA

1954–62 war of independence
1992 continuing internal conflic

WESTERN
SAHARA

1975–91
war of independence

## Government system 2001

- uncertain democracy
- monarchy
- dictatorship
- occupied territory
-  war *date shown*

### Degrees of freedom 2001

 not free  ◢ partly free

On the Freedom House 7-point system for measuring civil rights and political freedom, a score from 1 to 2.5 means the country can be considered "free", 3 to 5.5 means "partly free" and 5.5 and higher mean the country is "not free".

## Egypt

**1952** Gamel Nasser led a nationalist military coup against the pro-British king.
**1954** Nasser took the Suez Canal into national ownership.
**1956** British and French military intervention secretly coordinated with Israel failed to regain the Canal, partly because of American pressure.
**1967** Six Day War. Pre-emptive attack by Israel destroyed Egypt's air force in one day and took control of the Sinai Peninsula.
**1970** Nasser died, succeeded by Anwar Sadat.
**1973** Unsuccessful attempt to retrieve lost territory. Sadat later turned to diplomatic methods, resulting in a US-sponsored peace agreement with Israel in 1978 that demilitarised Sinai and returned it to Egypt. Other Arab states responded by expelling Egypt from the Arab League in 1979.
**1981** Sadat assassinated, succeeded by Hosni Mubarrak whose diplomacy helped Egypt back into the Arab League in 1989.
**1991** Egypt supported war against Iraq. Half its 20 billion dollar national debt was erased.
**1992** Gama'a al Islamiyya and other Islamist groups launch armed conflict with attacks on tourists, government officials, Coptic Christians and unveiled women. In one year, income from tourism fell by over 40 percent.
**1993** Bomb attack on the World Trade Center, New York, allegedly directed by Sheikh Omar Abedelrahman, the leader of Gama'a al Islamiyya.
**1997** Massacre at Luxor by Gama'a al Islamiyya: 62 people killed, 24 injured. The group claimed the attack was carried out to secure the release of Sheikh Abedelrahman. The massacre was the last major violence in the conflict.

## Tunisia

**1956** Independence from France, initially as a monarchy.
**1957** Republic founded under President Habib Bourguiba, who had led the independence struggle from 1934.
**1982** After their expulsion from Lebanon, PLO leader Yasser Arafat and several hundred PLO members were given refuge in Tunis and established new HQ. This was destroyed by an Israeli air raid in 1985.
**1984–85** Disturbance and instability over price rises and economic weakness; border tensions and clashes with Libya; rising influence of Islamist political groups.
**1987** Bourguiba declared medically unfit to govern and replaced by Zine al Abidine Ben Ali.
**1989** First free elections since 1956, Ben Ali's party wins all parliamentary seats. A crackdown on Islamist groups followed in 1990.
**1990–91** Ben Ali opposed both the Iraqi invasion of Kuwait and US-led offensive on Iraq.
**1999** Ben Ali re-elected President for third 5-year term, receiving 99 percent of the recorded vote.

## Libya

**1951** Independence: Libya had been an Italian possession from 1911 until World War Two, and was under British and French authority until independence.
**1969** Military coup led by Colonel Qadhafi overthrows monarchy. Qadhafi's radical foreign policy brought repeated military confrontations with the USA.
**1986** A bomb in a Berlin disco killed three people – two US servicemen and one Turkish woman – and injured 200. Ten days later, citing the Berlin bomb as justification, the USA bombed military installations and other targets in Libya, including Qadhafi's home, killing 30 people.
**1988** A civil American airliner exploded above Lockerbie, Scotland, killing 270 people. USA and Britain accused two Libyans of the plot and demanded they be tried in USA or Scotland.
**1990–91** Qadhafi opposed both the Iraqi invasion of Kuwait and US-led offensive on Iraq.
**1992** UN sanctions imposed on Libya for refusing to extradite two government officials for trial on Lockerbie bombing charges.
**1999** The two suspects were surrendered to UN authorities for a trial under Scottish law held on a military base in the Netherlands. UN sanctions on Libya were suspended but not formally lifted.
**2001** Lockerbie trial ended with one defendant convicted, one acquitted. Berlin disco trial ended with four defendants convicted – two Germans, one Palestinian, and one Libyan – and one acquitted.
**2002** Libya offered US$2.7 billion in compensation to families of Lockerbie victims.

◢ 6.5
T U N I S I A

▲ 7.7
L I B Y A

1995–97 internal conflict

▲ 6.5
E G Y P T

| 1948 | against Israel |
| 1956 | against Israel, Britain, France |
| 1967 | against Israel |
| 1973 | against Israel |
| 1992–97 | internal conflict |

# 27 | The Gulf

Politics in the Gulf are shaped by oil, by the widespread failure of democracy to take root, by the persistence of a few regimes that are capable of great cruelty, and by rivalries between the regional powers.

The need for oil has encouraged the USA and the West to trade, sell weapons and give political support to autocratic regimes.

In 1990 Iraq crossed the line of what the West could accept – not because it was a regime that tortures and summarily executes opponents, nor because of using chemical weapons against Kurdish villages and Iranian forces, and not because it was developing weapons of mass destruction. All these were cause for concern in western capitals but not for sanctions, isolation or war. Iraq crossed the line because it invaded Kuwait, thus threatening to destabilize world oil supplies.

Since the Gulf War of 1990-91 Iraq has been a pariah state. For a period, UN inspection teams were able to dismantle Iraqi capabilities for making long range and mass destruction weapons. Whether they did a comprehensive job has remained controversial since they were expelled in 1998.

Iran was isolated in the 1990s to only a slightly lesser degree, spurned because of its militant foreign policy, including extreme anti-American rhetoric as well as support for fighters against Israel in Lebanon, and because of its reluctance to disown the death sentence decreed without trial on a foreign author by the late Iranian religious leader, Ayatollah Khomeini. Strangely, it was when the militancy in foreign policy was being softened and there were signs of political reform within the country, that President Bush officially described Iran as evil.

Following the attacks on New York and the Pentagon on 11 September 2001, the US administration targeted Iraq as the next problem to deal with after al Qaida, believed responsible for the 11 September attacks. Battle plans were made – and leaked to the press in 2002 – before proof had been presented of a link between Iraq and al Qaida, or of Iraqi possession of mass destruction weapons.

As US pressure for war built up, other Arab states in the region were reluctant to support a new offensive against Iraq. Since

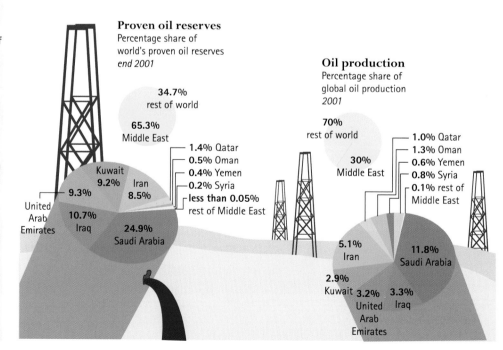

**Proven oil reserves**
Percentage share of world's proven oil reserves
*end 2001*

34.7% rest of world

65.3% Middle East

United Arab Emirates 9.3%
Kuwait 9.2%
Iran 8.5%
Iraq 10.7%
Saudi Arabia 24.9%

1.4% Qatar
0.5% Oman
0.4% Yemen
0.2% Syria
less than 0.05% rest of Middle East

**Oil production**
Percentage share of global oil production
*2001*

70% rest of world

30% Middle East

1.0% Qatar
1.3% Oman
0.6% Yemen
0.8% Syria
0.1% rest of Middle East

Iran 5.1%
Kuwait 2.9%
United Arab Emirates 3.2%
Iraq 3.3%
Saudi Arabia 11.8%

the first Gulf War, the US military presence in Saudi Arabia – the land where Islam began – has been regularly and scathingly criticized by al Qaida leader Osama bin Laden in his diatribes against corruption in the Arab world. A much wider band of opinion among Muslims is also outraged by the US presence there.

By mid-2002 Iraq's relations with the rest of the Arab world were warmer than at any point since 1989. There were the first signs of an easing of tensions between the old enemies Iran and Iraq as each tried to end their isolation. And there were concerns in world markets about what would happen to oil prices and the international economy in the event of war.

Few commentators doubted the USA could win a second Gulf War, but there were many questions about whether the war was justified or wise. But In November 2002, the UN voted to impose arms inspection and disarmament on Iraq, with serious consequences if Iraq cheated the inspectors again, as US war preparations continued. Meanwhile, outside powers jockeyed for a share of the post-war spoils of oil exploitation.

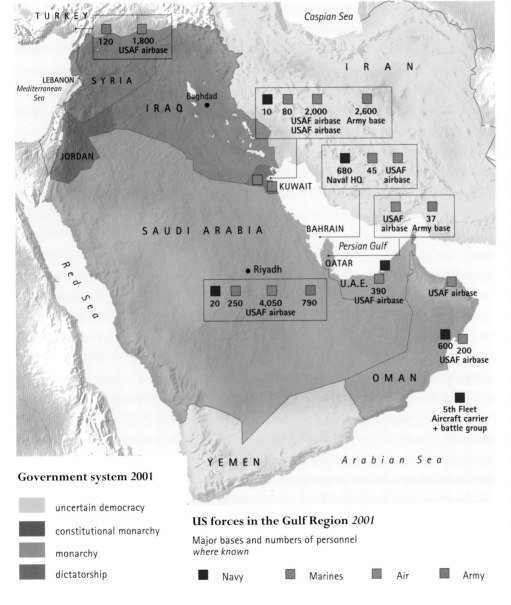

**Government system 2001**

- uncertain democracy
- constitutional monarchy
- monarchy
- dictatorship

**US forces in the Gulf Region** *2001*

Major bases and numbers of personnel *where known*

- Navy
- Marines
- Air
- Army

## IRAN

**1921** Army officer Reza Khan leads coup, become armed forces commander.
**1925** Reza Khan crowned Shah.

**1941** Britain and USSR invade Iran to protect supply routes; Reza Shah abdicates, his son Mohammad Reza Shah Pahlavi takes the throne.

**1951** Shah appoints as prime minister Mohammad Mossadeq – nationalist and proponent of taking oil into national ownership.
**1953** US and UK intelligence services organise overthrow of Mossadeq.

**1978** Growing unrest, emergence of opposition led from exile by Ayatollah Khomeini.
**1979** Shah leaves Iran, Khomeini returns, Islamic Republic of Iran established.
**1979–81** With official backing, Iranian students hold US diplomats hostage
**1980** War with Iraq. Covert arms supplies from US lead to scandal (Irangate).
**1988** War with Iraq ends.
**1989** Ayatollah Khomeini decrees a death sentence against British author Salman Rushdie for his novel, *The Satanic Verses*. Khomeini dies, succeeded as spiritual leader by Ayatollah Khamenei.

**1997** Reformist Muhammad Khatami elected President; extended dispute begins over acceptable degree of reforms.
**2002** Named by US President Bush as one of three states in an "axis of evil".

# CHAPTER SIX

# Asia

ASIA CONTAINS SEVERAL separate political and economic sub-regions. Among them there are profound differences in political system – from monarchy to democracy to Communist state – and likewise in the level of economic development and prosperity, and in current and recent experience of peace and war.

If there is one shared characteristic of many Asian wars, it is their longevity. Some wars do start and finish quickly, but many go on for over a decade. As a result, where the maps of Europe and the Middle East that open Chapters 4 and 5 show few current wars and many recent wars, the map of Asia here shows many current wars and rather few recently terminated ones.

One reason for this is that the governments of Burma, India and Indonesia have found it difficult or undesirable at times to treat all of their internal conflicts as wars in which it could be, in principle, possible to negotiate with an opponent. Where wars cannot be won they can only be ended by negotiation, which implies some degree of mutual acknowledgement as opponents. This minimal granting of status has often been impossible for leaders in South and Southeast Asia.

China spent the first half of the 20th century embroiled in internal armed conflict culminating in the Communist victory in 1949. Enforcing Tibet's inclusion within the People's Republic is the major conflict China has fought since 1950 inside its claimed international borders. There is also violence now in China's western province of Xinjiang. There have been conflicts with India and with Vietnam, and China remains involved in disputes over islands and reefs in the South China Sea. By comparison with 1900–1950, however, the world's most populous state has found peace under strong and authoritarian government; in a long historical perspective, such periods alternate with ones marked by internal wars. With a dynamic economy, an increasingly active diplomacy, and rapidly modernising armed forces, China has developed a world role.

Yet it is worth asking whether the internal peace can hold. Economic development in the last two decades has been spectacular but with many costs. It has been environmentally damaging and, as urban disasters remind us all too frequently, it has been full of corners cut and rules broken by get-rich-quick entrepreneurs. Although one group – the Han Chinese – constitute 90 percent of the population, China's national unity is in part an illusion. There are large regional, cultural and linguistic differences among the Han, major differences of class and access to wealth, with a wide gulf between the urban and rural populations.

The Chinese state apparatus is large, efficient and prepared to be ruthless. But long suppressed problems and tensions could yet erupt as explosively as they did in parts of the former USSR. Both for China and its neighbors, the consequences would then be hard to calculate.

Arctic Ocean

RUSSIA

KAZAKHSTAN

MONGOLIA

UZBEKISTAN

TURKMENISTAN

KYRGYZSTAN

TAJIKISTAN

AFGHANISTAN

PAKISTAN

NEPAL

BHUTAN

BANGLADESH

INDIA

CHINA

Arabian Sea

BURMA

LAOS

THAILAND

VIETNAM

CAMBODIA

SRI LANKA

NORTH KOREA

JAPAN

SOUTH KOREA

TAIWAN

Pacific Ocean

South China Sea

PHILIPPINES

Spratly Islands

BRUNEI

MALAYSIA

SINGAPORE

INDONESIA

EAST TIMOR

PAPUA NEW GUINEA

## Asian hotspots 2002

war

recent war *since 1990*

recent tension *since 1990*

**North Korea 2002**
Active nuclear weapons development program confirmed.

**1965** Second Kashmir War: India vs Pakistan.
**1967–68** China: Cultural revolution.
**1969–** India: Naxalites' guerrilla war.
**1969–** Philippines: Communist uprising and civil war.
**1970–98** Cambodia: civil war.
**1971** Pakistan: secession by Bangladesh, aided by India.
**1971** Sri Lanka: nationalist uprising.
**1973–77** Pakistan: civil war in Baluchistan.
**1973–97** Bangladesh: uprising in Chittagong Hill Tracts.
**1974–** Philippines: uprising in Mindanao.
**1975–99** East Timor: war of independence against Indonesia.

**1975–79** Vietnamese war with Cambodia.
**1975–90** Laos: civil war.
**1978–97** India: Nagaland uprising.
**1978–** Afghanistan: civil war (with Soviet intervention 1979–89, and US and allied intervention 2001– ).
**1979** Chinese-Vietnamese war.
**1981–93** India: Punjab uprising.
**1982–** India–Pakistan: Kashmir border war.
**1983–90** Sri Lanka: Nationalist uprising.

**1983–** Sri Lanka: Tamil uprising and civil war.
**1985–87** Chinese-Vietnamese border war.
**1987–** India: Uprising in Assam.
**1988–97** Papua New Guinea: Bougainville uprising.
**1989–** Indonesia: uprising in Aceh.
**1990–** India: uprising in Kashmir.

**1991–92** Burma: democratic uprising.
**1991–** India: Manipur uprising.
**1992–94** Burma: Arakan uprising.
**1992–98** Tajikistan: civil war.
**1992–** Burma: Kayah uprising.
**1992–** Pakistan: sectarian violence in Sind.

**1993–** India: Tripura uprising.
**1994–** Philipines: uprising in Mindanao.
**1996–** Pakistan: armed conflict in Punjab.
**1997–** Nepal: civil war.
**1999–** Indonesia: sectarian violence in Moluccan Islands.
**1999–** Uzbekistan: civil war.

73

# 28 Central Asia

The population of the five central Asian states consists of over 100 nationalities and ethnic groups. The borders between them were set in Moscow in the early days of the USSR. Though each republic as it was created was named after one nation, the borders between them had nothing to do with the boundaries between the areas where the major nationalities lived. For want of anything better, these borders persisted as the republics became independent states when the USSR broke up in 1991.

There was no push for independence in central Asia before the USSR broke up. The political elites were unprepared; there was no experience with either the institutions or the culture of democracy.

Since independence, progress towards democratic government is modest and economic development uncertain. Kazakhstan has the advantage of major oil deposits, though at less than one percent of world reserves and just on one percent of annual production, Kazakhstan's oil wealth will need to be used carefully if it is to be the basis of successful economic development.

Tajikistan descended into major war almost immediately. Fighting against the government was a coalition of groups variously calling themselves Islamic and democratic, but most analysts saw no clear ideological, ethnic or religious lines of division and conflict. Rather, the war was a battle between leaders in the different regions for control of the country's resources. Instability in Tajikistan both contributed to instability in neighbouring Afghanistan, and was itself made worse by events there. Large tracts of eastern Tajikistan remain essentially lawless today.

In Uzbekistan, the dividing lines are more clearly drawn, with several years of heavy handed attempts at controlling Islamist politics leading into armed conflict starting in 1999. The Islamist Movement of Uzbekistan (IMU) has had bases in both Afghanistan and Tajikistan and has fought much of its war in Kyrgyzstan.

The governments of Kyrgyzstan, Tajikistan and Uzbekistan all hoped that their willingness to let US and allied forces establish temporary air bases during the 2001-02 operations in Afghanistan would lead to favorable treatment from the West. They hoped this in turn would contribute to internal stability, while the expected US victory in Afghanistan might deliver a decisive blow against the IMU. Long term stability, however, requires sustainable development and democracy, not foreign military forces which, if they stay, will make tempting targets for IMU attacks and for heated rhetoric by ambitious opposition leaders.

The Fergana valley – with territory of all three states and a multi-ethnic population of five million – has been an object of anxiety for a decade. Violent clashes between different ethnic groups in 1989 and 1990 looked like the prelude to something a great deal worse. But through the first decade of independence, the explosion never came. The threat of water shortages is seen as a likely trigger for conflict over access to this vital natural resource. Peacebuilding efforts include work to improve water co-operation between the three states.

Neighboring the five central Asian states, and part of the region's strategic politics, is Xinjiang province, where, almost unseen by western eyes, the Uighur people have been struggling for cultural survival. Immigration has increased the proportion of Han (the ethnic majority in China) sevenfold in fifty years.

Among some militant groups, the struggle to keep an identity has been translated into a violent campaign for independence from China. Uighurs have been identified in Afghanistan among al Qaida forces and at religious schools in Pakistan, but there is no convincing evidence of a large scale militant Islamism in Xinjiang, and no evidence of al Qaida or IMU activity inside China.

Before the USA had declared global war on terrorism, China had declared regional war on Islamic radicalism. The Shanghai Cooperation Organization – China, Kazakhstan, Kyrgyzstan, Russia, Tajikistan, Uzbekistan – is setting up an anti-terrorist coordinating center in the Kyrgyzstan capital of Bishkek.

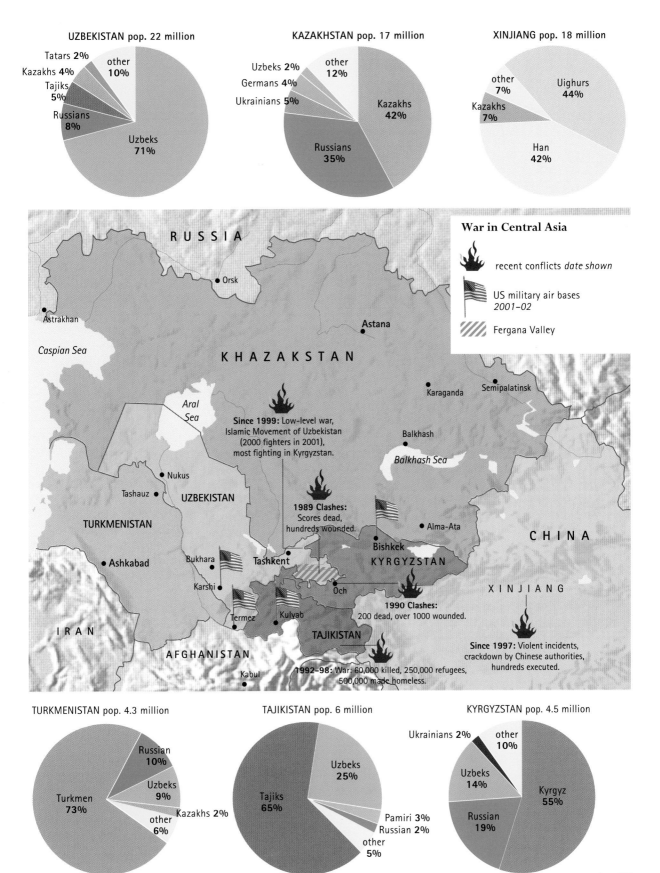

**UZBEKISTAN pop. 22 million**

Tatars **2%**
Kazakhs **4%**
Tajiks **5%**
Russians **8%**
other **10%**
Uzbeks **71%**

**KAZAKHSTAN pop. 17 million**

Uzbeks **2%**
Germans **4%**
Ukrainians **5%**
other **12%**
Kazakhs **42%**
Russians **35%**

**XINJIANG pop. 18 million**

other **7%**
Kazakhs **7%**
Uighurs **44%**
Han **42%**

**War in Central Asia**

recent conflicts *date shown*

US military air bases *2001–02*

Fergana Valley

RUSSIA

• Orsk

• Astrakhan

*Caspian Sea*

• Astana

K H A Z A K S T A N

*Aral Sea*

• Karaganda

• Semipalatinsk

• Nukus

• Tashauz

UZBEKISTAN

**Balkhash**

*Balkhash Sea*

**Since 1999:** Low-level war, Islamic Movement of Uzbekistan (2000 fighters in 2001), most fighting in Kyrgyzstan.

TURKMENISTAN

• Ashkabad

Bukhara •

Tashkent

**1989 Clashes:** Scores dead, hundreds wounded.

• Alma-Ata

Bishkek

K Y R G Y Z S T A N

C H I N A

Karshi •

Och •

**1990 Clashes:** 200 dead, over 1000 wounded.

X I N J I A N G

IRAN

Termez •

Kulyab •

TAJIKISTAN

**Since 1997:** Violent incidents, crackdown by Chinese authorities, hundreds executed.

AFGHANISTAN

Kabul •

**1992–98:** War: 60,000 killed, 250,000 refugees, 500,000 made homeless.

**TURKMENISTAN pop. 4.3 million**

Russian **10%**
Uzbeks **9%**
Turkmen **73%**
Kazakhs **2%**
other **6%**

**TAJIKISTAN pop. 6 million**

Uzbeks **25%**
Tajiks **65%**
Pamiri **3%**
Russian **2%**
other **5%**

**KYRGYZSTAN pop. 4.5 million**

Ukrainians **2%**
other **10%**
Uzbeks **14%**
Russian **19%**
Kyrgyz **55%**

# 29 | Afghanistan

The communist coup against President Daoud in 1978 ushered in an era of total war in Afghanistan. When the USSR invaded, its leaders believed they were starting a swift operation to put a new leader from the rival communist faction in power and stabilise the country. This blunder into disaster became part of the reason for the USSR's break-up.

When the USSR withdrew in 1989, war deaths amounted to 1.5 million and there were 6 million refugees. The war then entered a new and more violent phase. The pro-Soviet government hung on for three years before the *mujaheddin* took Kabul, formed a new government, and promptly went to war on each other. The Taliban emerged dramatically in 1994 with the conquest of Kandahar, took the capital two years later, and by the middle of 2001 were in control of most of the country. The murder of their most effective military opponent – Ahmad Shah Massoud, leader of the Northern Alliance – in September of that year seemed likely to confirm their victory. In the 12 years of war after the Soviet withdrawal, the death toll was at least half a million.

Taliban rule was notable for extreme repression of women, for public executions and mutilations of criminals, for arbitrary punishments, and for punishment of anyone who expressed any thoughts that deviated from those of the Taliban leader, Mullah Omar. All this was justified by religious interpretations shaped by local traditions, in ways that were not only narrow-minded but also contested by most Muslims.

The swift identification of Osama bin Laden and the al Qaida network as responsible for the attacks on the USA on 11 September 2001 took the Afghan war into a third phase. The overthrow of the Taliban was efficiently accomplished, but all the problems and contending forces created by two decades of war remained at work.

Afghanistan is ethnically divided. The Taliban are largely Pashtun, their opposition largely Tajik and Hazara. Afghan politics is characterized by a confusing mixture of deep ethnic loyalties and a willingness by some to sell out anybody for the right price.

Afghanistan is a major narcotics producer. Its share of worldwide opium production rose from 40 percent in 1988 to a peak of 80 percent in 1999. Production dropped in 2000 after the Taliban imposed a characteristically effective ban on growing new poppies. Though the western-backed President, Hamid Karzai, imposed a total ban on every aspect of opium production and trade in 2002, his writ is less effective than was Mullah Omar's. Production for 2002 was expected to be at about the level of the mid-1990s, around half of world output.

The reason President Karzai's power is limited is that the US war on the Taliban was fought through warlords. It is they who have power in Afghanistan, each running his region as a medieval kingdom, and for some, opium is merely easy profit.

"Warlord" is an over-used term but in Afghanistan it has real meaning. The current Hazara military leader Ismail Khan led an uprising against Soviet influence in 1979. Ahmad Shah Massoud, the assassinated leader of the Northern Alliance, was among the leaders of an attempted Islamic uprising against President Daoud in 1975. Alongside him then was his later rival Gulbuddin Hekmatyar, whose artillery tortured Kabul from 1993 to 1995. Rashid Dostum, whose forces accomplished key victories on the road to overthrowing the Taliban, led an anti-*mujaheddin* force in 1989, defecting from the communist government in its death throes in 1992. And Mullah Omar and Osama bin Laden themselves reportedly escaped the US offensive in December 2001, and their forces were still active in 2002.

These men are indeed lords of war. They and their lesser brethren are the real political and military forces in Afghanistan, especially outside Kabul. They know only one way to be sure they get what they want. While their power persists, Afghanistan and its people face perpetual risk of total war.

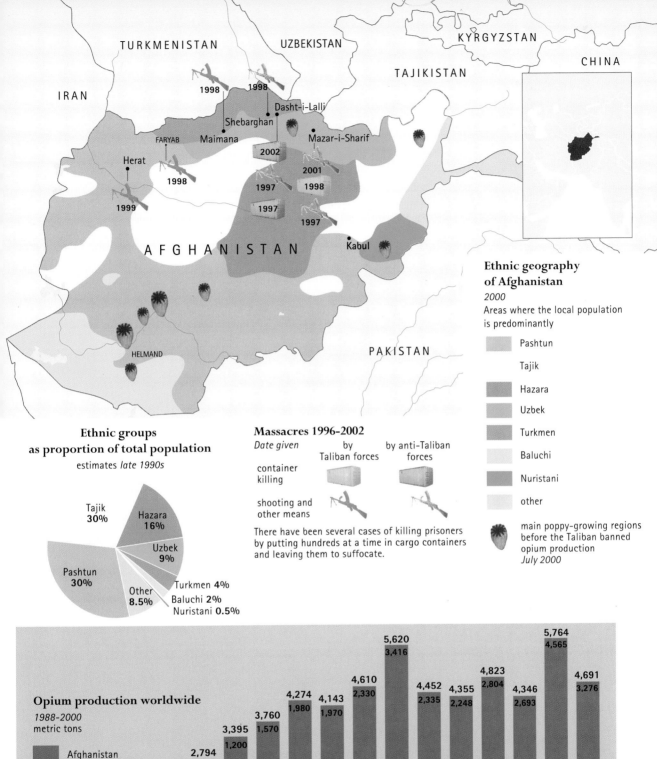

TURKMENISTAN UZBEKISTAN KYRGYZSTAN

TAJIKISTAN

CHINA

IRAN

**1998** **1998**

Dasht-i-Lalli

Shebarghan

FARYAB Maimana

Herat

**2002**

Mazar-i-Sharif

**1998**

**1999**

**2001**

**1997** **1998**

**1997**

**1997**

A F G H A N I S T A N

Kabul

HELMAND

PAKISTAN

### Ethnic geography of Afghanistan

*2000*
Areas where the local population is predominantly

- Pashtun
- Tajik
- Hazara
- Uzbek
- Turkmen
- Baluchi
- Nuristani
- other

main poppy-growing regions before the Taliban banned opium production
*July 2000*

### Ethnic groups as proportion of total population

estimates *late 1990s*

Tajik 30%
Hazara 16%
Uzbek 9%
Pashtun 30%
Other 8.5%
Turkmen 4%
Baluchi 2%
Nuristani 0.5%

### Massacres 1996-2002

*Date given*     by Taliban forces     by anti-Taliban forces

container killing

shooting and other means

There have been several cases of killing prisoners by putting hundreds at a time in cargo containers and leaving them to suffocate.

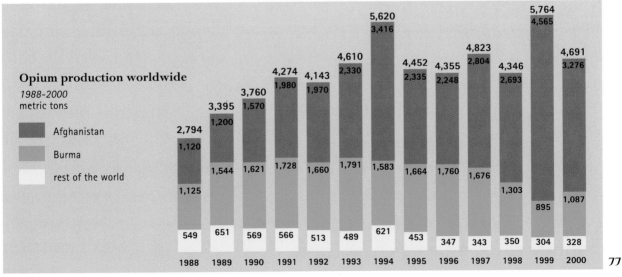

### Opium production worldwide

*1988-2000*
metric tons

- Afghanistan
- Burma
- rest of the world

| Year | Total | Afghanistan | Burma | rest of the world |
|---|---|---|---|---|
| 1988 | 2,794 | 1,120 | 1,125 | 549 |
| 1989 | 3,395 | 1,200 | 1,544 | 651 |
| 1990 | 3,760 | 1,570 | 1,621 | 569 |
| 1991 | 4,274 | 1,980 | 1,728 | 566 |
| 1992 | 4,143 | 1,970 | 1,660 | 513 |
| 1993 | 4,610 | 2,330 | 1,791 | 489 |
| 1994 | 5,620 | 3,416 | 1,583 | 621 |
| 1995 | 4,452 | 2,335 | 1,664 | 453 |
| 1996 | 4,355 | 2,248 | 1,760 | 347 |
| 1997 | 4,823 | 2,804 | 1,676 | 343 |
| 1998 | 4,346 | 2,693 | 1,303 | 350 |
| 1999 | 5,764 | 4,565 | 895 | 304 |
| 2000 | 4,691 | 3,276 | 1,087 | 328 |

77

mountainous terrain across a provisional border that neither one accepts, where they have fought two major wars and gone through two decades of confrontation and on-off clashes.

Pakistan was created as a state for Muslims; India's founders wanted ethnic and religious pluralism. From these different starting points both countries have arrived at the edge of religious warfare.

When the two countries became independent in 1947, they were partitioned from each other and there was a huge population exchange during which over one million people died. Among the arrivals in

Kashmir is the world's most dangerous region. Here, two unstable societies, one governed by a military dictatorship, the other plagued by multiple internal wars, both with powerful armed forces, each with nuclear capability, confront each other in

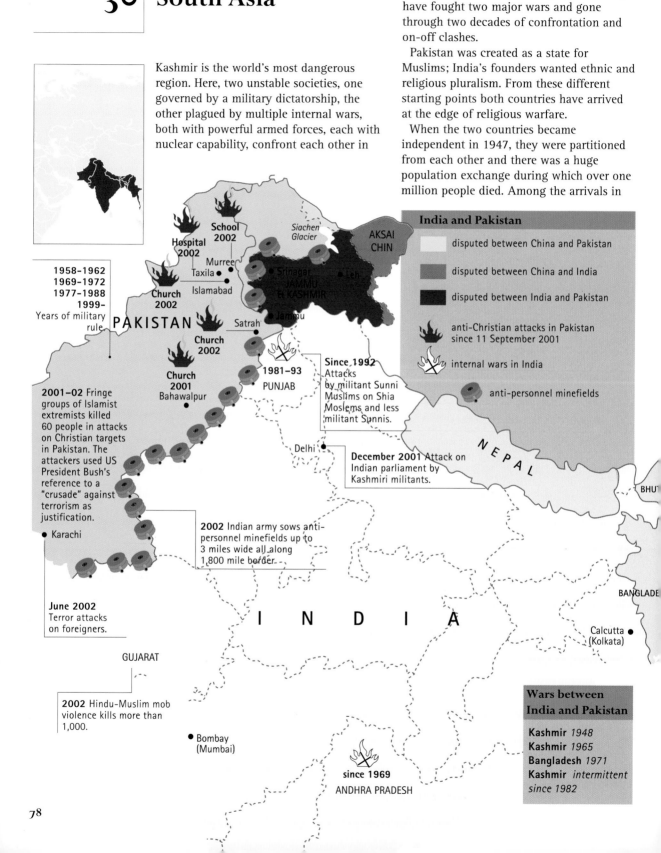

**India and Pakistan**

- disputed between China and Pakistan
- disputed between China and India
- disputed between India and Pakistan

anti-Christian attacks in Pakistan since 11 September 2001

internal wars in India

anti-personnel minefields

School 2002
Hospital 2002
Murree
Taxila
Church 2002
Islamabad
Satrah
Church 2002
Church 2001
Bahawalpur
Karachi

Siachen Glacier
AKSAI CHIN
Srinagar
JAMMU & KASHMIR
Leh
Jammu

PAKISTAN

**1958–1962
1969–1972
1977–1988
1999–**
Years of military rule

**2001–02** Fringe groups of Islamist extremists killed 60 people in attacks on Christian targets in Pakistan. The attackers used US President Bush's reference to a "crusade" against terrorism as justification.

**June 2002** Terror attacks on foreigners.

GUJARAT

**2002** Hindu-Muslim mob violence kills more than 1,000.

**1981–93**
PUNJAB

**Since 1992** Attacks by militant Sunni Muslims on Shia Moslems and less militant Sunnis.

Delhi

**December 2001** Attack on Indian parliament by Kashmiri militants.

**2002** Indian army sows anti-personnel minefields up to 3 miles wide all along 1,800 mile border.

NEPAL

BHU

BANGLADE

Calcutta (Kolkata)

I N D I A

Bombay (Mumbai)

since 1969
ANDHRA PRADESH

**Wars between India and Pakistan**

**Kashmir** *1948*
**Kashmir** *1965*
**Bangladesh** *1971*
**Kashmir** *intermittent since 1982*

Pakistan from India were the Deobandi religious schools. In the 1990s these provided recruits for the Taliban in Afghanistan, and from them come some of the militants involved in sectarian violence within Pakistan.

In India there are over 100 million Muslims. The Gujarat riots in February 2002 demonstrated once again the potential vulnerability of Muslims in India where Hindu opinion is liable to be inflamed by fears about Pakistan's intentions in Kashmir, by the support it provides for anti-Indian insurgents, and by its financial and practical support for the Taliban since 1994.

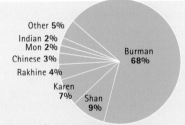

### Ethnic groups in Burma

*Lack of firm census data means there is no reliable picture of Burma's ethnic make-up. The chart shows the generally accepted rough estimates.*

## Burma: State of permanent war

The Burmese dictatorship likes to lie, even in the name it gives itself – having come to power by coup in 1988 it called itself the State Law and Order Restoration Council, and in 1997 renamed itself the State Peace and Development Council. In fact there is permanent war, poverty is widespread and economic development only benefits a minority. There are over a million refugees within Burma's borders and about 400,000 in neighboring countries. There are 50,000 child soldiers, 1,800 political prisoners and unknown millions of men, women and children in forced labor.

In 1990, the National League for Democracy won the elections with 82 percent of the vote. The League's leader, Aung San Suu Kyi, was put under house arrest. In 2002, for the second time since her incarceration began, house arrest was lifted and the regime showed interest in negotiating with her.

## Nepal: War since 1996

War deaths *1996-2002*: approximately 4,000

areas effectively controlled by Communist Party of Nepal-Maoist *mid 2002*

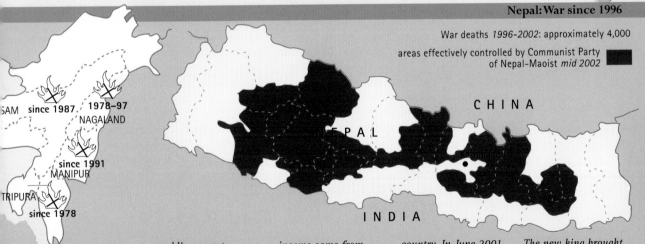

The Nepalese monarchy's limited experiment with democracy began in 1990. But democracy neither made the economy more productive nor led to a more even distribution of wealth. In one of the world's poorest countries, the poor got even poorer as a new political class successfully purloined some of the limited national wealth. In 2002, 43 percent of the population lived below the poverty line; 60 percent of national income came from external aid.

A Maoist-led insurgency started in 1996. In the first five years, about 2,000 people died in guerrilla attacks and fighting between the insurgents and the police, mostly in remote rural areas of the country. In June 2001, the Crown Prince slaughtered most of the royal family. The murders were committed in the haze of a drunken quarrel and appear to have had no connection to the political, economic and security crisis of the country.

The new king brought the army into the war. As a result, in the ensuing year, the war spread to about 80 percent of the country, the insurgents expanded their areas of effective control, and the rate of killing accelerated fivefold.

# 31 | Sri Lanka

During the British Raj, the Tamil minority of the colony then called Ceylon took up a proportion of government posts that was larger than its percentage in the population, and was likewise disproportionately prominent among businessmen. Soon after independence in 1948, the resentment that this kind of ethnic advantage provoked became a factor in Sri Lankan politics.

In the 1956 elections, both the main Sinhalese parties promised that Sinhalese would become the only official language. The winning party's platform was "Sinhala only". The main Tamil party's platform demanded a separate Tamil-language region with a federal Sri Lanka.

Violence erupted in the form of inter-communal riots in 1958, leaving hundreds dead, mostly Tamils, following rumours that a Tamil had killed a Sinhalese. In the early 1960s, there was renewed and worsening inter-communal violence as the "Sinhala only" policies were implemented.

By the 1977 elections, the main Tamil party was demanding independence and terrorism had been started by the Liberation Tigers of Tamil Eelam (LTTE, usually known as the Tamil Tigers), beginning with the murder of the mayor of Jaffna. Immediately after the elections, rumours that Tamil terrorists had killed Sinhalese policemen led to 300 deaths in inter-communal rioting. Further rioting in 1983 claimed 400 lives, many of them specifically targeted by well organised groups identifying Tamil names and addresses on voter registration lists. In this six year period 1977-83 Sri Lanka slid into open civil war that, by 2002, had cost over 60,000 lives.

The Tamil Tigers pioneered large scale suicide bombing. Against this, alongside conventional military operations, the Sri Lankan army has developed the use of hit squads penetrating deep into Tamil territory.

In February 2002 the government of Sri Lanka and the Tamil Tigers signed a ceasefire agreement. The previous ceasefire lasted only four months in 1995. The 2002 ceasefire agreement, brokered by the Norwegian government, included detailed clauses on the steps each side would take, measures to maintain calm and build confidence, and a process for monitoring compliance. But the technical strength of the agreement only emphasised the importance of the big question, whether both sides were committed to finding the compromises needed to end their bitter war.

The Norwegian government continued its role as the talks moved from ceasefire arrangements to discussing a final settlement. But as the talks were under way in Thailand in November, discussing power-sharing arrangements, a court in Colombo sentenced *in absentia* the Tigers' leader Vellupillai Prabhakaran to 200 years in jail for conspiracy in a 1996 bombing that killed nearly 100 people. And observers wondered whether the Sri Lankan President, herself badly wounded in a Tamil Tiger suicide bombing in 1999, would attempt to stop the Prime Minister – from the rival Sinhalese party – proceeding with the negotiations.

---

### Prominent murders

*The Liberation Tigers of Tamil Eelam have, among others, killed*
- *One president of Sri Lanka*
- *One former prime minister of India*
- *2 Sri Lankan government ministers*
- *14 Members of Parliament*
- *6 mayors, former mayors and deputy mayors*
- *6 leaders of political parties*
- *8 other prominent Sri Lankan politicians*

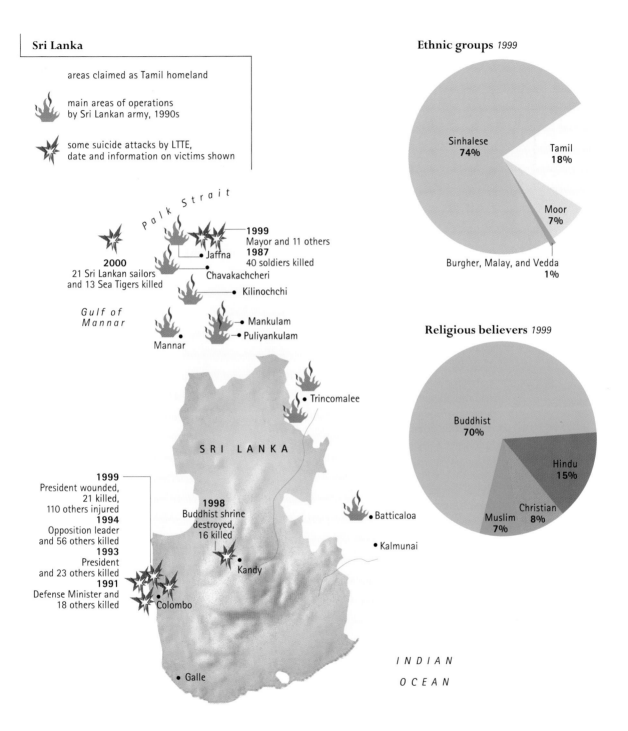

**Sri Lanka**

areas claimed as Tamil homeland

main areas of operations
by Sri Lankan army, 1990s

some suicide attacks by LTTE,
date and information on victims shown

*Palk Strait*

**1999**
Mayor and 11 others
**1987**
40 soldiers killed

Jaffna

**2000**
21 Sri Lankan sailors
and 13 Sea Tigers killed

Chavakachcheri

*Gulf of
Mannar*

Kilinochchi

Mankulam
Puliyankulam

Mannar

Trincomalee

S R I   L A N K A

**1999**
President wounded,
21 killed,
110 others injured
**1994**
Opposition leader
and 56 others killed
**1993**
President
and 23 others killed
**1991**
Defense Minister and
18 others killed

**1998**
Buddhist shrine
destroyed,
16 killed

Batticaloa

Kalmunai

Kandy

Colombo

*INDIAN*

*OCEAN*

Galle

**Ethnic groups** *1999*

Sinhalese
**74%**

Tamil
**18%**

Moor
**7%**

Burgher, Malay, and Vedda
**1%**

**Religious believers** *1999*

Buddhist
**70%**

Hindu
**15%**

Christian
**8%**

Muslim
**7%**

# 32 | Southeast Asia

War in Southeast Asia has come in overlapping waves. First came the independence wars in the 1940s and 1950s, against the French in Indochina and the British in Malaysia (then Malaya). Then in the 1960s and 1970s, came wars that were part of the global confrontation between the US and Soviet alliance systems – Vietnam and Cambodia, Indonesia where half a million Communists were massacred as the pro-West Suharto dictatorship took control in 1966, and the Philippines where a Communist insurgency started in 1969.

In the third wave of wars, starting in the 1970s, the key issue has been control of natural resources, though the parties often divided along ethnic lines.

Indonesia, the region's most populous country, and the world's most populous Islamic country, began a transition away from dictatorship in 1998. With over 700 langauges in daily use and a matching cultural diversity despite the unifying element of Islam (about 85 percent of the population are Muslim), its size and island geography make Indonesia a perfect candidate for division and separation. While the changes in Indonesia have brought an end to the conflict over East Timor, with great pain along the way, they have also generated new violence, not least in the Moluccan Islands. To bring stability out of the chaos of the turn of the century will take great stores of political wisdom, goodwill and luck.

In the Philippines, a long Islamist insurrection in the resource-rich island of Mindanao turned into a campaign of terror and counter-terror at the end of the 1990s. The Abu Sayyaf group is notorious both for its kidnappings and for receiving training from al Qaida. Following the destruction of al Qaida's main bases in Afghanistan, there were reports and rumours that some al Qaida fighters had relocated to Indonesia and the Philippines.

## Cambodia

War started as a sideshow to the war in Vietnam. In 1975 the Communist Khmer Rouge were victorious, and then went to war against the population. Massacres and famine marked the KR's rule, killing at least two million. In 1978 Vietnam overthrew the KR, but guerrilla war continued. A peace agreement in 1991 began the process of ending the war. Fighting continued after the agreement but a UN peacekeeping force successfully organized and monitored elections under fire in 1993. Slowly the KR's strength dwindled and in 1998 the remnants surrendered.

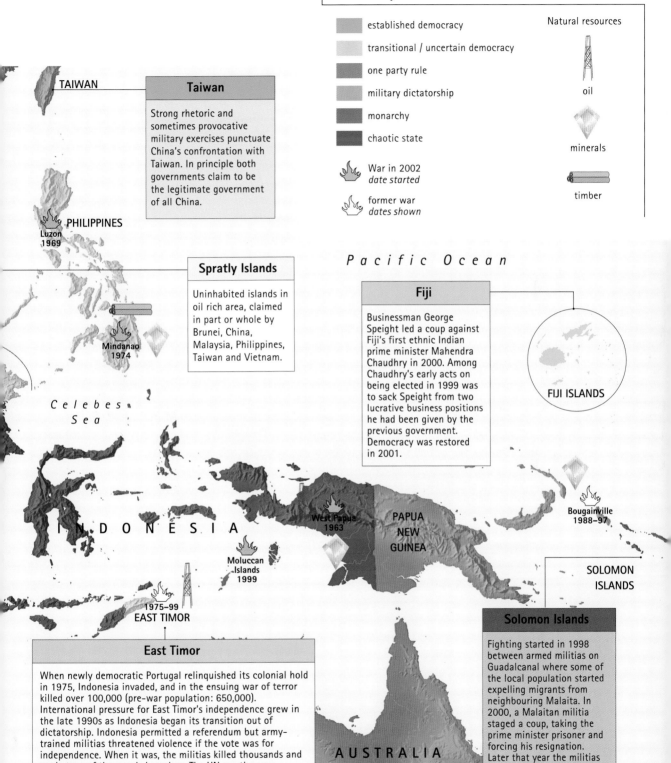

## Political systems *2002*

- established democracy
- transitional / uncertain democracy
- one party rule
- military dictatorship
- monarchy
- chaotic state

War in 2002
*date started*

former war
*dates shown*

Natural resources

oil

minerals

timber

*Pacific Ocean*

TAIWAN

### Taiwan

Strong rhetoric and sometimes provocative military exercises punctuate China's confrontation with Taiwan. In principle both governments claim to be the legitimate government of all China.

PHILIPPINES

Luzon
1969

### Spratly Islands

Uninhabited islands in oil rich area, claimed in part or whole by Brunei, China, Malaysia, Philippines, Taiwan and Vietnam.

Mindanao
1974

*C e l e b e s
S e a*

### Fiji

Businessman George Speight led a coup against Fiji's first ethnic Indian prime minister Mahendra Chaudhry in 2000. Among Chaudhry's early acts on being elected in 1999 was to sack Speight from two lucrative business positions he had been given by the previous government. Democracy was restored in 2001.

FIJI ISLANDS

I N D O N E S I A

West Papua
1963

PAPUA
NEW
GUINEA

Bougainville
1988–97

SOLOMON
ISLANDS

Moluccan
Islands
1999

1975–99
EAST TIMOR

### Solomon Islands

Fighting started in 1998 between armed militias on Guadalcanal where some of the local population started expelling migrants from neighbouring Malaita. In 2000, a Malaitan militia staged a coup, taking the prime minister prisoner and forcing his resignation. Later that year the militias signed a peace agreement, which has lasted though tensions and grievances remain.

### East Timor

When newly democratic Portugal relinquished its colonial hold in 1975, Indonesia invaded, and in the ensuing war of terror killed over 100,000 (pre-war population: 650,000). International pressure for East Timor's independence grew in the late 1990s as Indonesia began its transition out of dictatorship. Indonesia permitted a referendum but army-trained militias threatened violence if the vote was for independence. When it was, the militias killed thousands and made tens of thousands homeless. The UN ran the new country until 2001 elections produced an independent government. The fate of up to 80,000 refugees who were forced into West Timor remained unknown.

AUSTRALIA

# CHAPTER SEVEN

# Africa

IN 2002, NEW STATISTICS led to predictions of the HIV/AIDS pandemic causing 68 million deaths worldwide by 2020, 55 million of them in sub-Saharan Africa. The expected sub-Saharan African death toll is approximately the same as the death tolls – both civilian and military – in World War One and World War Two combined. Among young adults, aged 15-24, the infection rate is between two and three times as high for women as for men.

The link between conflict and HIV/AIDS is two-way: the virus is a threat to peace and is spread particularly by war.

War creates conditions that accelerate the spread of disease – poverty, famine, physical destruction of health facilities and of clean water supply, large population movements. As a sexually transmitted disease, the acceleration of the spread of HIV/AIDS by war is related to changes in behavior, to an increased willingness to take risks among people living in extreme conditions, and to the movement of large numbers of people as refugees or soldiers.

Forced out of their homes by conflict, and often sexually assaulted, young women may be forced into prostitution, or find that is the only way to obtain money, food or medicines. Some African armies have very high HIV/AIDS infection rates – about 40 percent in South Africa, up to 60 percent in Angola and the Democratic Republic of the Congo, as high as 75 percent in Zimbabwe.

These factors combine to suggest that the estimates of HIV/AIDS infection in some of Africa's war-torn countries may mask the extent of the problem; DRC, Rwanda, Sudan, Sierra Leone and Liberia – together with Nigeria whose army has undertaken peacekeeping interventions in the wars in Sierra Leone and Liberia – could all be close to the edge of a major increase in reported rates of infection.

HIV/AIDS is a threat to peace because, affecting populations on such a large scale, it attacks the national ability to generate wealth and run complex, developing societies. Education suffers, home life suffers, working life suffers, government administration suffers. The epidemic thus strengthens the socio-economic patterns of deprivation and a badly functioning economy that are associated with the onset of social instability, violence and armed conflict: income growth per person in sub-Saharan Africa is being cut by about 0.7 percent a year because of the epidemic.

HIV/AIDS is first and foremost a human tragedy – and more tragic because it is a preventable tragedy – but of such dimensions that it adds up to a national disaster and a danger to regional prosperity and stability.

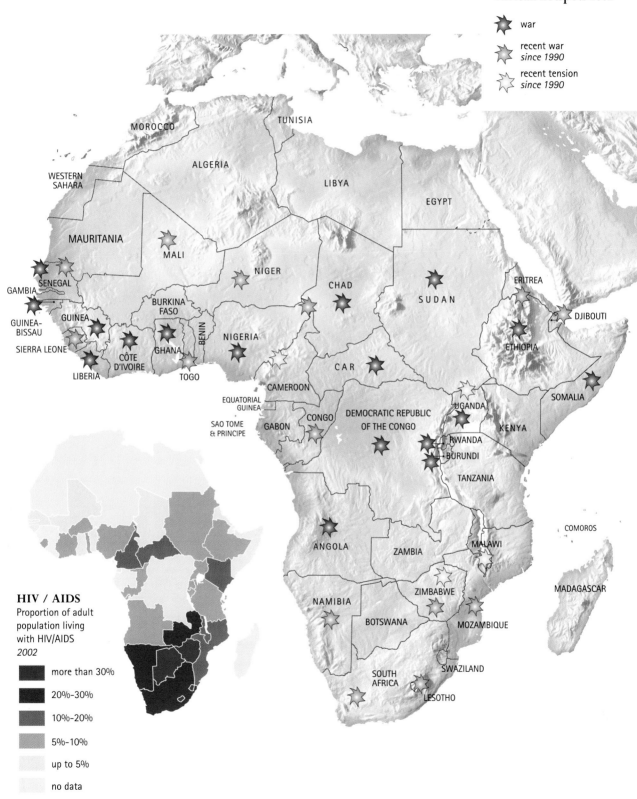

African hotspots 2002

- ⭐ war
- ⭐ recent war *since 1990*
- ☆ recent tension *since 1990*

MOROCCO
WESTERN SAHARA
TUNISIA
ALGERIA
LIBYA
EGYPT
MAURITANIA
MALI
NIGER
CHAD
SUDAN
ERITREA
DJIBOUTI
SENEGAL
GAMBIA
GUINEA-BISSAU
GUINEA
BURKINA FASO
BENIN
NIGERIA
ETHIOPIA
SIERRA LEONE
CÔTE D'IVOIRE
GHANA
TOGO
LIBERIA
CAMEROON
C A R
SOMALIA
EQUATORIAL GUINEA
SAO TOME & PRINCIPE
GABON
CONGO
DEMOCRATIC REPUBLIC OF THE CONGO
UGANDA
KENYA
RWANDA
BURUNDI
TANZANIA
COMOROS
ANGOLA
ZAMBIA
MALAWI
MADAGASCAR
NAMIBIA
ZIMBABWE
MOZAMBIQUE
BOTSWANA
SOUTH AFRICA
SWAZILAND
LESOTHO

**HIV / AIDS**
Proportion of adult
population living
with HIV/AIDS
*2002*

- more than 30%
- 20%–30%
- 10%–20%
- 5%–10%
- up to 5%
- no data

85

# 33 Colonial History and Dispossession

In the last 20 years of the 19th century, Europeans conquered 85 percent of Africa. After not much more than 50 years, the Europeans decided they could not exploit Africa efficiently enough to make it worth their while to stay. Starting in 1955, in a period of 25 years, European governments returned control of 80 percent of Africa to Africans.

There is no historical parallel for such an abrupt process of colonial conquest and decolonization. Widespread warfare and poverty show that the continent and its people have never recovered.

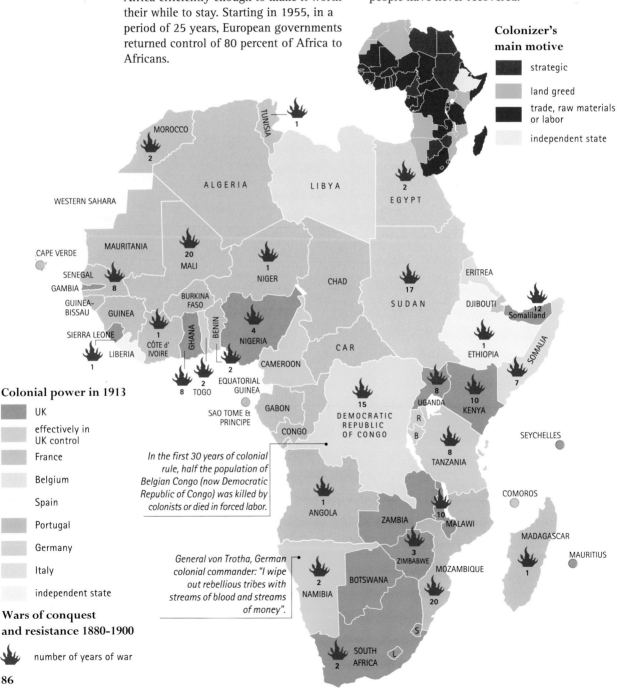

**Colonizer's main motive**
- strategic
- land greed
- trade, raw materials or labor
- independent state

**Colonial power in 1913**
- UK
- effectively in UK control
- France
- Belgium
- Spain
- Portugal
- Germany
- Italy
- independent state

**Wars of conquest and resistance 1880-1900**

🔥 number of years of war

*In the first 30 years of colonial rule, half the population of Belgian Congo (now Democratic Republic of Congo) was killed by colonists or died in forced labor.*

*General von Trotha, German colonial commander: "I wipe out rebellious tribes with streams of blood and streams of money".*

MOROCCO 2
TUNISIA 1
ALGERIA
LIBYA
EGYPT 2
WESTERN SAHARA
MAURITANIA
CAPE VERDE
SENEGAL 8
GAMBIA
GUINEA-BISSAU
GUINEA
SIERRA LEONE 1
LIBERIA 1
MALI 20
NIGER 1
BURKINA FASO
CÔTE d' IVOIRE 1
GHANA
BENIN
TOGO 2
NIGERIA 4
EQUATORIAL GUINEA 2
CHAD
SUDAN 17
CAR
CAMEROON 8
GABON
SAO TOME & PRINCIPE
CONGO
DEMOCRATIC REPUBLIC OF CONGO 15
ERITREA
DJIBOUTI
Somaliland 12
ETHIOPIA 1
SOMALIA 7
UGANDA 8
KENYA 10
R B
TANZANIA 8
SEYCHELLES
ANGOLA 1
ZAMBIA
MALAWI 10
COMOROS
ZIMBABWE 3
MOZAMBIQUE
MADAGASCAR 1
MAURITIUS
NAMIBIA 2
BOTSWANA
SOUTH AFRICA 2
S L 20

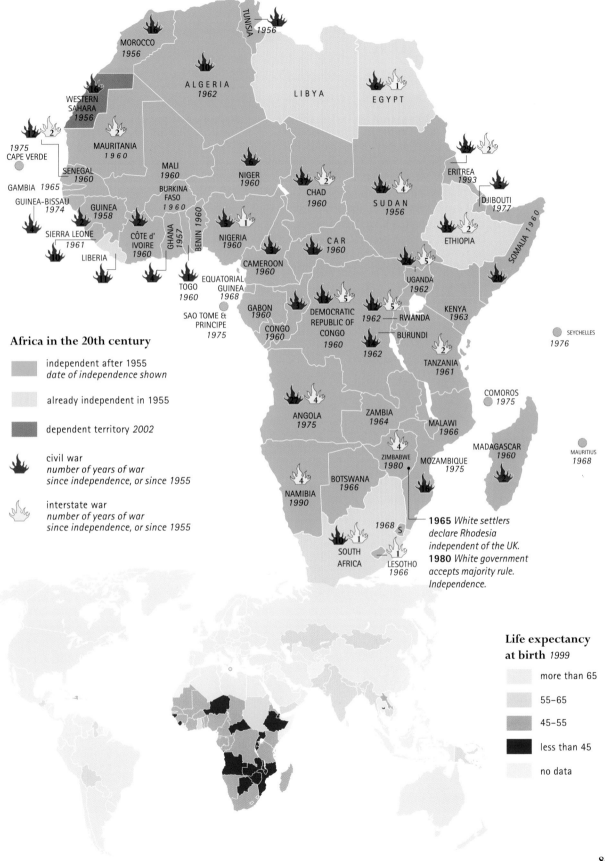

## Africa in the 20th century

TUNISIA *1956*

MOROCCO *1956*

WESTERN SAHARA *1956*

ALGERIA *1962*

LIBYA

EGYPT

*1975* CAPE VERDE

MAURITANIA *1960*

MALI *1960*

NIGER *1960*

CHAD *1960*

SUDAN *1956*

ERITREA *1993*

DJIBOUTI *1977*

SENEGAL *1960*

GAMBIA *1965*

GUINEA-BISSAU *1974*

BURKINA FASO *1960*

BENIN *1960*

GUINEA *1958*

SIERRA LEONE *1961*

CÔTE d' IVOIRE *1960*

GHANA *1957*

LIBERIA

TOGO *1960*

NIGERIA *1960*

CAMEROON *1960*

C A R *1960*

ETHIOPIA

SOMALIA *1960*

EQUATORIAL GUINEA *1968*

SAO TOME & PRINCIPE *1975*

GABON *1960*

CONGO *1960*

DEMOCRATIC REPUBLIC OF CONGO *1960*

RWANDA *1962*

BURUNDI *1962*

UGANDA *1962*

KENYA *1963*

TANZANIA *1961*

SEYCHELLES *1976*

ANGOLA *1975*

ZAMBIA *1964*

MALAWI *1966*

COMOROS *1975*

MADAGASCAR *1960*

MAURITIUS *1968*

ZIMBABWE *1980*

MOZAMBIQUE *1975*

NAMIBIA *1990*

BOTSWANA *1966*

SOUTH AFRICA

LESOTHO *1966*

S

**1965** *White settlers declare Rhodesia independent of the UK.* **1980** *White government accepts majority rule. Independence.*

independent after 1955
*date of independence shown*

already independent in 1955

dependent territory *2002*

civil war
*number of years of war since independence, or since 1955*

interstate war
*number of years of war since independence, or since 1955*

## Life expectancy at birth *1999*

more than 65

55–65

45–55

less than 45

no data

# 34 West Africa

West Africa has never recovered from colonial rule. Though rich in natural resources, no country in the region has managed to generate a reasonable degree of prosperity for the majority of its citizens. Corruption and the abuse of power are rife, and democracy is rare, and weak and unstable at best. Many of the leaders who can claim to have been elected were put in power through fraud and intimidation, showing again that elections are not always democratic.

The HIV/AIDS pandemic is weakening the region's already poor development prospects. HIV spreads rapidly in war for several reasons. Because of their risk-taking behavior, the infection rate for military personnel in Africa is twice the rate for the civilian population. In addition, war escalates sexual violence: it is used as a tactic by some forces in order to spread terror, and refugee populations are vulnerable to all kinds of exploitation including rape. Young girls made homeless and parentless by war may see little option but prostitution if they are to survive. And when peace comes and the international peacekeepers arrive, the number of prostitutes usually increases to meet the increased demand.

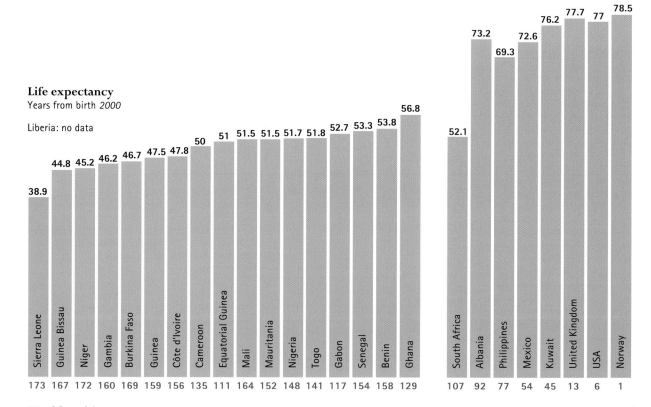

**Life expectancy**
Years from birth *2000*

Liberia: no data

| Country | Life expectancy | World ranking |
|---|---|---|
| Sierra Leone | 38.9 | 173 |
| Guinea Bissau | 44.8 | 167 |
| Niger | 45.2 | 172 |
| Gambia | 46.2 | 160 |
| Burkina Faso | 46.7 | 169 |
| Guinea | 47.5 | 159 |
| Côte d'Ivoire | 47.8 | 156 |
| Cameroon | 50 | 135 |
| Equatorial Guinea | 51 | 111 |
| Mali | 51.5 | 164 |
| Mauritania | 51.5 | 152 |
| Nigeria | 51.7 | 148 |
| Togo | 51.8 | 141 |
| Gabon | 52.7 | 117 |
| Senegal | 53.3 | 154 |
| Benin | 53.8 | 158 |
| Ghana | 56.8 | 129 |
| South Africa | 52.1 | 107 |
| Albania | 73.2 | 92 |
| Philippines | 69.3 | 77 |
| Mexico | 72.6 | 54 |
| Kuwait | 76.2 | 45 |
| United Kingdom | 77.7 | 13 |
| USA | 77 | 6 |
| Norway | 78.5 | 1 |

**World ranking**
Position in the UN Human Development Index of 173 countries *2002*

## Debt versus health

National wealth spent on paying interest on debt compared to proportion spent on health.
*All West African governments spend less on caring for the health of their citizens than on paying the interest on debts to foreign bankers.*

- more than 6 times greater
- between 2 and 6 times greater
- up to 2 times greater
- no data

- armed conflict active 2000-2002
- armed conflict active at any time in 1990s but not in 2000s
- elected government 2002
- non-elected government 2002

### Gambia
Independent 1965. First direct elections for president 1982. Military coup 1994. Return to civilian rule 1996.

### Mauritania
Independent 1960. One-party state or military dictatorship 1964-92.

Fighting with Senegal 1989-91 triggered by disputes over access to grazing land and water resources.

### Niger
Independent 1960. Democracy until 1974. Military rule until 1989 – first elections 1993. Political instability 1995 ended by military coup 1996, new elections. New constitution 1999.

War 1991-97 triggered by Touareg resentment of ill treatment of those returning to Niger after fleeing the Sahelian drought 1968-74.

### Guinea-Bissau
Independent 1974. First multi-party elections 1994.

Attempted military coup 1998, became protracted civil war.

### Senegal
Independent 1960. One party state 1966-78.

War with Casamance separatists since 1990. Border war Mauritania 1989-91.

### Mali
Independent 1960. Dictatorship till 1991.

1990-95 Touareg separatism.

### Guinea
Independent 1958. One party state until 1992.

Caught between wars in Liberia and Sierra Leone, war came to Guinea in late 2000 with attacks by Liberian forces on Liberian rebels' bases and by dissidents supported by the Liberian government and Sierra Leonean rebels.

### Burkina Faso
Independent 1960, military in power for most of the period since. Presidential election 1998.

### Benin
Independent 1960. Military rule 1965-8 and 1969-70. One-party rule 1974-91.

### Nigeria
Independent 1960. Military rule 1966-79 and 1993-99.

Intense fighting and communal fighting in north since 2000 about introduction of Islamic Sharia law.

### Sierra Leone
Independent 1991. One party system 1978-96.

Civil war 1991-2002. Revolutionary United Front uprising may have had no aims other than control of the diamond trade. The RUF's trademarks included child soldiers, and rule by terror based on mass rape and amputating hands or feet of their opponents and victims. War ended by intervention of UN peacekeeping force and British combat forces.

### Liberia
Independent since being founded in 1847. Decades of tightly limited democracy led into a decade of dictatorship from 1980, and a period of no effective government from 1990-97.

Civil war from 1989 to 1997 ended with election of the leader of the strongest armed force in the country. War returned to northern regions in 1999 with attacks by rebels from bases in Guinea.

### Côte-d'Ivoire
Independent 1960. One-party state until 1990. Military dictatorship 1999-2000. Further coup attempt 2001.

Political chaos deepened inter-ethnic disputes, consolidating into civil wars.

### Ghana
Independent 1957. Military rule 1966-69, 1972-9 and 1981-92.

Inter-ethnic conflict in the north in 1994-95 and sporadic violence in the north east since 1999, triggered by land disputes.

### Togo
Independent 1960. Military rule 1967-92. Former head of military government still President following elections in 1998 declared fraudulent by outside observers.

Fighting in 1991.

### Cameroon
Independent 1960. Effectively one-party state 1966-90.

### Equatorial Guinea
Independent 1968. One-party state 1970-79; military dictatorship until 1983; return to one-party rule till 1993. Opposition parties persistently harassed.

### Gabon
Independent 1960. One-party system 1968-91.

# 35 | The Congo

Democratic Republic of the Congo (DRC) has copious natural resources. As well as oil, minerals, coal, precious metals and diamonds, DRC is home to 50 percent of Africa's forests (6 percent of the world total) and in its rivers there is 50 percent of Africa's hydro-electric capacity (13 percent of the world total).

Not once since independence in 1960 – and certainly not before then, in a colonial regime that was unremittingly brutal – have the ordinary people of the country been able to share in its wealth. Instead, the national riches have been a source of personal wealth for a few and the lure for the involvement of outside powers. The multiple external military interventions in DRC since the late 1990s have further sapped the country's wealth.

In 1997, Rwanda and Uganda helped Laurent Kabila into power. In 1998, finding him not pliable enough, they promoted a second uprising to remove him. Other African states stepped in to block these ambitions. In four years of war, over two million people died – about half a million killed in the fighting, and about two million dying from preventable diseases and war-induced starvation. By the end of the war in 2002, at least two million people had been forced out of their homes and remained unable to return. Most of these were out of the reach of humanitarian aid workers.

The health system in DRC was in a state of total collapse by war's end. Outbreaks of meningitis, cholera, measles and malaria are common, and the incidence of sleeping sickness, tuberculosis, and HIV/AIDS is

## One country – many names

Congo Free State – 1885

Belgian Congo – 1908

Congo – 1960

Zaire – 1971

Democratic Republic of the Congo – 1997

---

**1885** King Leopold II of Belgium acquires the Congo Basin under the Treaty of Berlin. Procedes to exploit so-called Congo Free State as private possession. Under his control, half the population was killed or died in forced labor. Punishments for those who did not work hard enough included amputating their hands.

**1908** Belgian government takes control of the colony and re-names it Belgian Congo.

**1959** Riots in Léopoldville. Belgian government announces intention to grant Congo independence. In a population of 14 million, there were 17 university graduates, no doctors, lawyers or engineers.

**1960** June: Independence. The rival leaders of the two main independence movements, Kasa-Vubu and Patrice Lumumba, become President and Prime Minister respectively.

July: Army mutiny. The two richest provinces (Katanga and Kivu) seceded. Belgian troops briefly intervene to protect Belgian interests, leading to heavy fighting. Lumumba calls in the UN.

September: Kasa-Vubu fires Lumumba and is in turn impeached by Parliament. Army Chief of Staff Colonel Joseph Mobutu seizes control. Lumumba arrested and handed over to the leader of the Katangese gendarmes who beat him to death. The UN's failure to restore order, despite a force ranging in size from 15,000 to 20,000 troops, leads to a crisis during which the USSR announces it no longer recognises the authority of the UN Secretary-General Dag Hammarskjold, who later dies in September 1961 in an air crash widely suspected to be not accidental.

**1961** Mobutu returns Kasa-Vubu to power.

**1962–63** UN forces suppress the Katanga insurrection.

**1965** Mobutu takes power in a bloodless military coup and defeats remaining pro-secession forces in south.

**1971** Country renamed Zaire.

**1972** Mobutu changes his name to Mobutu Sese Seko.

**1994** Civil war in Rwanda; genocide against Tutsis. Refugee crisis. Mobutu allows Hutu refugees to settle in UN camps in eastern Zaire. Tensions and violence grow between Hutu militias and Zairean Tutsis.

**1996–97** Tutsi uprising against Mobutu, starting in Kivu province, led by Laurent Kabila, and supported by Rwanda and Uganda. Kabila's forces reportedly murder thousands of Hutus during his short and victorious war. Mobutu dies in exile in

September 1997. Country renamed the Democratic Republic of Congo (DRC).

**1998** New Tutsi uprising, again with backing from Rwanda and Uganda, joined later by Burundi, this time against Kabila. Angolan, Chadian, Namibian and Zimbabwean forces intervene to keep Kabila in power, later with Sudanese help.

**2000** Fighting starts between Rwandan and Uganda forces inside DRC.

**2001** Laurent Kabila assassinated. His son, Joseph Kabila, takes power and opens peace talks. Peace agreements signed in July 1999 and December 2000 but fighting continues.

**2002** Further peace agreement. Most foreign troops begin withdrawal. Stability of agreement uncertain.

rising rapidly. A single Congolese doctor typically serves 25,000 people. One in four children die before reaching the age of five. Less than half of the population has access to clean drinking water. Average life expectancy is 45.

## Congo (Brazzaville)

A French colony from 1891 to 1960, Congo (Brazzaville) emerged from one-party rule in 1992 for a brief period of uncertain democracy. Civil war broke out in 1997. After five months of fighting, Denis Sassou-Nguesso, who had been President 1979-91, took power again. Fighting continued for two more years. In 2000 Sassou-Nguesso promised to restore democracy.

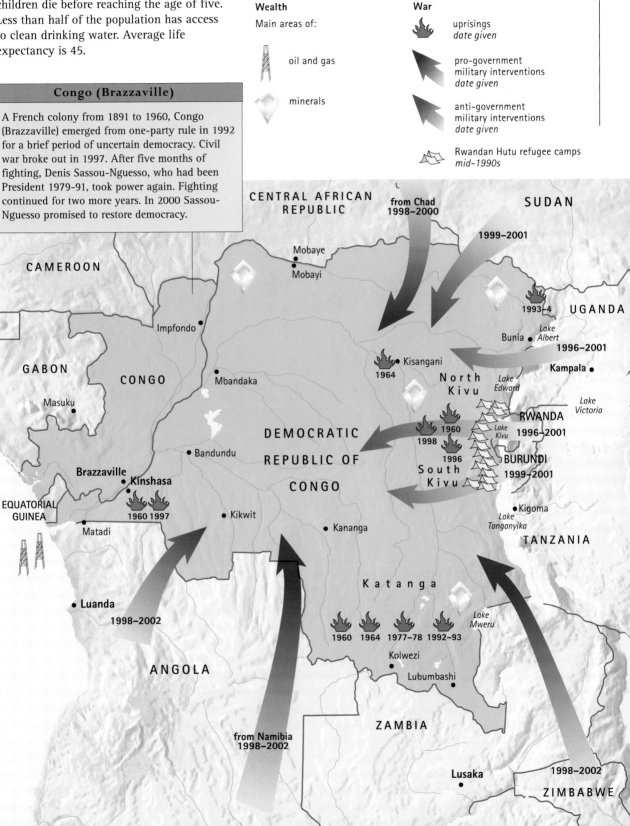

### Wealth and war in the Democratic Republic of the Congo

**Wealth**
Main areas of:

oil and gas

minerals

**War**

🔥 uprisings
*date given*

◄ pro-government military interventions
*date given*

◄ anti-government military interventions
*date given*

Rwandan Hutu refugee camps
*mid-1990s*

# 36 Burundi and Rwanda

**1890s** Burundi and Rwanda incorporated into German East Africa.
**1915–16** Belgian colonial forces from neighboring Congo push German forces out.
**1923** Belgium receives League of Nations mandate to govern Burundi and Rwanda
(changed after World War Two to United Nations Trust). Belgian authorities govern through the Tutsi local rulers.
**1959–61** Hutu uprising in Rwanda deposes Tutsi king and establishes republic.
**1962** Burundi and Rwanda are made separate independent countries.

## BURUNDI

**1962** Fearing an uprising by the Hutu majority as in Rwanda, Tutsi leaders strike pre-emptively, attacking potential opponents and Hutu leaders.
**1965** The king ignores election results giving Hutu parties a majority in national assembly and appoints a Tutsi prime minister. Unsuccessful coup attempt by Hutu officers comes close enough to success that the king flees.
**1966** Monarchy replaced by republic controlled by Tutsi leader President Micombero.
**1972** Hutu uprising, government reprisals.
**1976** Bloodless coup: Micombero is ousted and replaced by President Bagaza.
**1981** New constitution declares Burundi a one-party state.
**1980s** Increasing tension between church and state, harassment of clergy, growing authoritarianism of Bagaza's government.
**1987** Bagaza overthrown and replaced by President Buyoya, head of junta.
**1988** Resentment at treatment by local Tutsi officials in northern Burundi sparks Hutu uprising, followed by army reprisals. Buyoya responds by appointing a Hutu prime minister and preparing a transition to democracy.

**1992** New constitution introduces multi-party system; failed coup attempt, apparently instigated by Bagaza while in exile in Libya.
**1993** June: First democratic elections bring a Hutu to the presidency, Melchior Ndadye, with a power sharing government; a Tutsi woman, Sylvie Kinigi is appointed prime minister. October: Military coup, Ndadye is assassinated; open warfare starts.
**1994** February: New president, also a Hutu.
**1995** Renewed violence in Bujumbura. June: Presidents of both Burundi and Rwanda killed when their plane is shot down near Kigali. September: Third Hutu President in a year is appointed with coalition government.
**1996** Buyoya returns to power in military coup.
**1998** Buyoya sworn in as President as transitional constitution is agreed.
**1999** Ceasefire talks.
**2000** Ceasefire agreement; fighting continues.
**2001** After two failed coup attempts, talks brokered by Nelson Mandela lead to agreement on 3-year transitional power-sharing government under Buyoya. At the end of the year the fighting intensifies again.

## RWANDA

**1963** Army of Tutsi exiles start uprising, government reprisals.
**1973** Military coup led by General Habyarimana.
**1978** New constitution: Habyarimana confirmed in power for five more years (re-elected 1983, 1988).
**1990** Rwandan Patriotic Front (mostly but not exclusively Tutsi) crosses border from Uganda to open uprising.
**1991** New multi-party constitution.
**1992** Ceasefire/peace talks open.
**1993** Peace accord signed in Arusha, Tanzania: they call for power-sharing government and inclusion of Tutsis in senior army positions. UN peacekeeping mission starts.
**1994** April-July: President Habyarimana and his Burundi counterpart are killed when their plane is shot down near Kigali. An RPF military unit stationed in Kigali under the Arusha accord comes under attack and RPF launches new offensive. Hutu army and militias launch evidently prepared reprisals. RPF takes Kigali and expels Hutu army and militias. Tutsi retaliation for Hutu killings starts. 20,000 Hutu refugees die in cholera epidemic in refugee camps. July: Ceasefire, new government formed with moderate Hutu President.

**1996** Expelled Hutu militias organize attacks into Rwanda from Zaire. RPF and Zairean Tutsis launch attacks on militias in and around Hutu refugee camps in Zaire. End of UN peacekeeping mission in Rwanda. RPF begins process of trying over 120,000 people for offenses related to 1994 massacre.
**1997** International Criminal Tribunal working in Arusha begins trials. Hutu militias attack Tutsi civilians. Rwanda broadens its military activities in Zaire into supporting, with Ugandan aid, an uprising led by Laurent Kabila that overthrows the Mobutu government.
**1998** Because of continuing action by Hutu militia in re-named DRC, Rwanda with Uganda attempt to overthrow Kabila.
**2000** Paul Kagame, military leader of RPF, becomes Rwanda's first Tutsi president.
**2001** To accelerate trials for the 1994 offenses, Rwandan government turn to traditional court system in which ordinary people judge their peers.

In 1994, in one of the worst acts of genocide the world has ever seen, 800,000 Rwandans were killed in a six week period. The victims were mostly Tutsi – the minority ethnic group in Rwanda, as in neighboring Burundi – but there were also many Hutus – the majority group in both countries – who opposed the policies of the Hutu government.

Nothing was done to prevent the massacre because the UN failed to read the warning signs, which to close observers were many and obvious. An official international study of the failure was scathing, for the Hutu-Tutsi rivalry has spawned massacres and mass flight in both countries during four decades.

In Burundi, leaders of the Tutsi minority have ruled for most of the period since independence; in Rwanda, leaders of the Hutu majority. The rivalry of the two groups has become a byword for bitter ethnic hatred. Yet the differences between the two groups are small – they share the same religions, for example, and there are many other similarities. Like many such rivalries, this is fundamentally a question of power, and the problem is that political leaders have found it possible to strengthen their power through actively emphasising all the differences and none of the commonalities between the two groups.

## Uganda

*Uganda's history since the 1980s has been marked by an uphill effort to recover from the effects of the previous decade. Idi Amin, who took power in 1971, ruled at the cost of at least 100,000 Ugandan lives until his invasion of Tanzania in 1978 led to a counter-invasion the following year and his exile. Instability and civil war cost about 300,000 lives before The National Resistance Army won and installed Yoweri Museveni as president in 1986. Civil wars have continued since then, most persistently in the north where the Christian fundamentalist Lord's Resistance Army operates from bases in Sudan.*

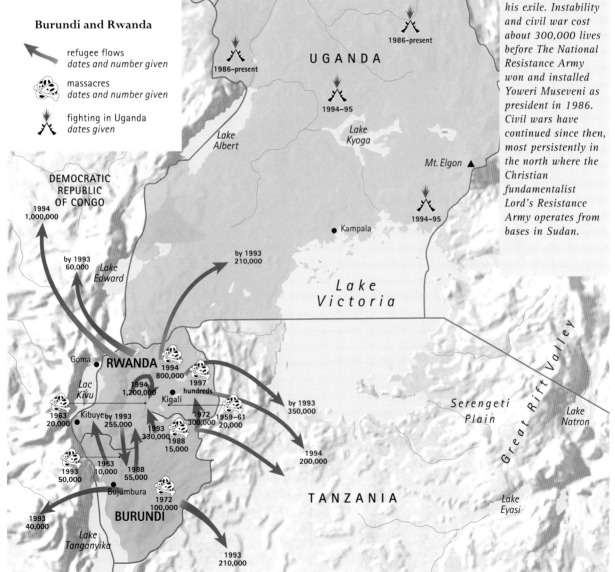

### Burundi and Rwanda

refugee flows
*dates and number given*

massacres
*dates and number given*

fighting in Uganda
*dates given*

93

# Horn of Africa

Since the early 1960s, over three million people have died in wars in the Horn of Africa. During the 1980s, famine took one million lives in Ethiopia alone – and the famine was itself part of the war – the chronic shortages of food, leading to starvation and the denial of humanitarian assistance to people in need, were the deliberate strategy of the Ethiopian regime of the time. The poverty of the Horn is partly the cause of armed conflicts and partly the consequence. The countries of the region have spent decades trapped in a repetitive cycle of frustration, instability, repression and violence.

Eritrea was united with Ethiopia in a federation in 1952 by decision of the United Nations. A decade later, the Ethiopian ruler Haile Selassie did away with the fiction of federation and made Eritrea a province. The uprising began and became a war of independence, helping weaken the Selassie regime and preparing the way for a military coup to depose him in 1974 after widely supported strikes and demonstrations.

The new ruling military junta, known as the Derg, quickly became more repressive and more feared and hated than the previous regime. Faced with a militant campaign to undermine its authority, the Derg responded with a campaign of terror that killed 100,000 people in 1977 and 1978.

The Eritrean independence fighters made common cause with those struggling for freedom within Ethiopia and in 1991 the Derg was finally overthrown. Eritrea went on to have a referendum and secure its independence in 1993.

The year 1991 should have been a year of hope for the Horn, for not only was the Derg overthrown but also, after a 14 year war,

Siad Barre the Somalian dictator was also defeated. But in Somalia the victors immediately fell out, in Ethiopia the peace was only an interlude, while in Djibouti a five year war started.

In Somalia a series of inter-factional fights started in 1991, turning into all-out war and generalized chaos, leading to famine, controversial and unsuccessful military intervention by the USA, and an equally unsuccessful attempt at peacekeeping by the UN. After the interventions were over, the fighting continued. Successive attempts to bring the factions to negotiations have been partially successful, but there have always been a few faction leaders for whom the greater profit seems to lie in continued warfare.

In Ethiopia low-level conflict started up again by the mid-1990s, but the most serious blow to the hopes generated by the victory of 1991 came in 1998 when Eritrea and Ethiopia went to war over an arid area on their mutual border where the precise dividing line had not been properly delineated at the moment of independence. Hundreds of thousands of soldiers were poured into offensives and counter-offensives, and hundreds of thousands of lives were lost in a territorial conflict between two of the world's poorest countries. An agreement in 2000 brought the war to an end and, despite serious tensions in the following year, in 2002 both countries officially accepted a new border drawn by an independent commission.

If the two governments will allow themselves to have peaceful relations with each other, both may have the chance to get on with addressing the development problems their people face.

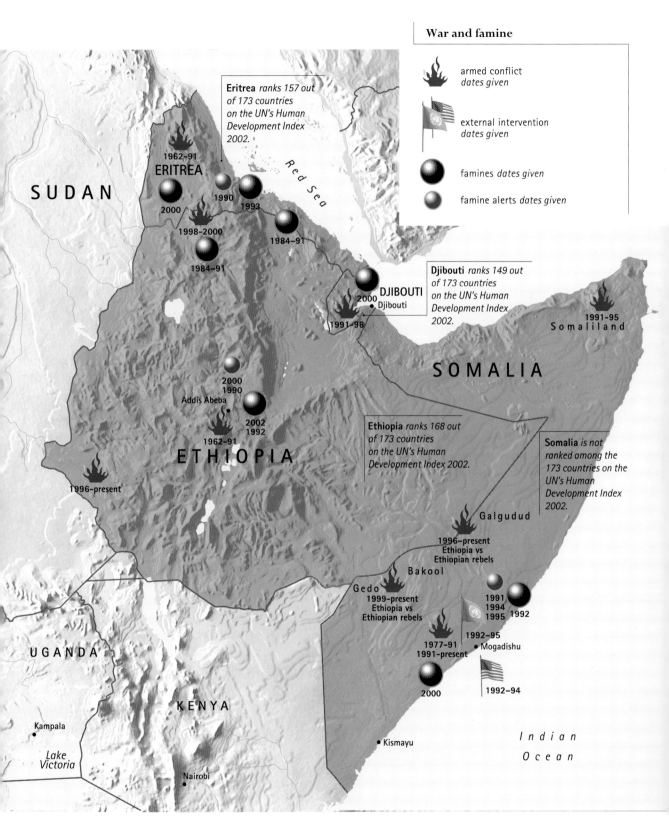

## War and famine

⚔ armed conflict
*dates given*

🏴 external intervention
*dates given*

● famines *dates given*

• famine alerts *dates given*

**SUDAN**

**Red Sea**

1962–91
**ERITREA**
2000    1990
1993

1998–2000

1984–91

1984–91

*Eritrea ranks 157 out of 173 countries on the UN's Human Development Index 2002.*

2000
**DJIBOUTI**
• Djibouti

1991–96

*Djibouti ranks 149 out of 173 countries on the UN's Human Development Index 2002.*

1991–95
**Somaliland**

**SOMALIA**

2000
1990
• Addis Abeba
2002
1992

1962–91

**ETHIOPIA**

1996–present

*Ethiopia ranks 168 out of 173 countries on the UN's Human Development Index 2002.*

*Somalia is not ranked among the 173 countries on the UN's Human Development Index 2002.*

**Galgudud**

1996–present
Ethiopia vs
Ethiopian rebels

**Bakool**

**Gedo**

1999–present
Ethiopia vs
Ethiopian rebels

1977–91
1991–present

1991
1994
1995

1992

1992–95
• Mogadishu

2000

1992–94

**UGANDA**

• Kampala

*Lake Victoria*

**KENYA**

• Nairobi

• Kismayu

*Indian Ocean*

# 38 Sudan

In Sudan there are 19 major ethnic groups and 597 subgroups, speaking over 100 languages and dialects. To hold such a diverse country together would require wisdom, tolerance, a successful development strategy and good luck. None of these have been present since independence in 1956, when Sudan was already embroiled in an internal war as leaders in the south sought autonomy.

In 1972, a peace deal was arranged. It lasted eleven years. War re-started in 1983, over the same issues, when a group of army officers rebelled and formed the Sudanese People's Liberation Army.

Estimates of war deaths in the two decades since then range from 1.2 million to over 2 million. There are approximately 4 million displaced people. Many have been forced to abandon their homes more than once. In the south, it is estimated that 80 percent of the population has been displaced at least once.

Direct combat between government forces and the SPLA is rare. Instead, while the SPLA launches guerrilla raids on government targets and supply lines, government forces attack civilians in the south to weaken the base of support for the SPLA.

Among its tactics, the government has bombed villages indiscriminately, used famine as a weapon, forced civilians to flee, and supported militia forces engaging in the slave trade. Tens of thousands of civilians have been enslaved, though the government has repeatedly denied it.

The SPLA and its allied militias have also attacked civilian areas indiscriminately and have forced civilians – including children – into military service for them.

The return to war was sparked in 1983 by the government's decision to impose Islamic Shari'a law. This is the basis of a general impression that the war is about the ethnic and religious difference between the largely Arab and Muslim north of the country and the south, which is black African with traditional animist religious beliefs and a Christian minority. But this general impression is wrong. In 1991, Shari'a law was removed from the south, but the war continued.

The population is not divided just one way. There is much racial diversity among the Arabs of the north, despite their common language and religion. Their ways of life are very different depending on whether they are city dwellers, village farmers or nomads. Among Africans in the south, differences are equally important, and took political form in the early 1990s when the SPLA split and there was severe combat between largely Dinka and largely Nuer groups.

Though cultural difference and religious freedom are important, the war is mainly about the control of territory and its resources, and about successive governments in Khartoum exploiting the south's resources but failing to help it develop economically.

When the Derg was defeated in Ethiopia in 1991, the SPLA lost one of its key backers. The government of Sudan was then able to encourage internal division and faction fighting within the SPLA. It could not

## Ethnic geography of Sudan

*FUR* predominant ethnic group

Arabic speaking area

achieve decisive victories in the field, however, and the war continued.

The government came to power in a coup in 1989. Seeking a leading international role in militant Islamist politics, it played host to Osama bin Laden as he built up the al Qaida network. International pressure on the regime led it to tell bin Laden to leave Sudan in 1996. US suspicions of Sudanese complicity in terrorism in 1998 led to a missile strike on a factory in Khartoum.

In the 1990s, oil reared its head. So that international corporations can develop oil extraction in the south, government-backed militias have been clearing civilian populations out of the way, using terror and wholesale destruction of property. When a Swedish oil company made a test drilling in April 1999 and confirmed that the oil could be profitably exploited, tens of thousands of people were forced out of their homes in the vicinity. Further north where Canadian investments have been made, large areas of territory were laid waste and depopulated. Oil income allows the government to arm

itself more strongly with the aim of pursuing the war more successfully. In response, the SPLA launched attacks on the infrastructure of oil extraction.

The SPLA increased the pressure on the Khartoum government through making alliances both with other groups from all parts of the country in a National Democratic Alliance and, in January 2002, with a rival militia force, the Sudan People's Defence Force. The government then agreed to a temporary ceasefire in the Nuba Mountains and against all odds this was followed in July 2002 by a meeting mediated by Ugandan President Museveni between Sudanese President al Bashir and SPLA leader John Garang. The meeting produced a framework agreement to end the war. In October 2002 there was a further ceasefire agreement, but the first accusations that it was being violated came only a week later.

## Oil concessions in central and southern Sudan

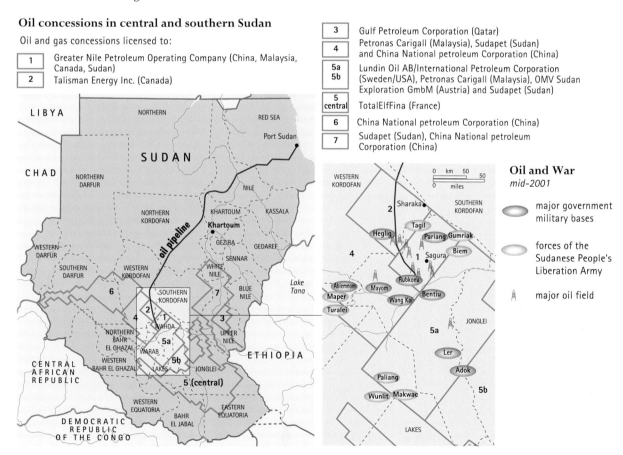

Oil and gas concessions licensed to:

| 1 | Greater Nile Petroleum Operating Company (China, Malaysia, Canada, Sudan) |
| 2 | Talisman Energy Inc. (Canada) |

| 3 | Gulf Petroleum Corporation (Qatar) |
| 4 | Petronas Carigall (Malaysia), Sudapet (Sudan) and China National petroleum Corporation (China) |
| 5a 5b | Lundin Oil AB/International Petroleum Corporation (Sweden/USA), Petronas Carigall (Malaysia), OMV Sudan Exploration GmbM (Austria) and Sudapet (Sudan) |
| 5 central | TotalElfFina (France) |
| 6 | China National petroleum Corporation (China) |
| 7 | Sudapet (Sudan), China National petroleum Corporation (China) |

**Oil and War**
*mid-2001*

- major government military bases
- forces of the Sudanese People's Liberation Army
- major oil field

97

# 39 | Southern Africa

In two decades, hopes for the region of southern Africa have soared from the lowest to the highest and plummeted down again. Seemingly endless wars gave way to an era of peacemaking and growing democracy, only for AIDS to emerge as a threat to life, to development and to peace.

Armed conflict dominated the region in the 1980s. In South Africa the apartheid system entered its most repressive phase with an escalation of conflict both within the country and outside it, as the white regime attacked its foes throughout the region. In Namibia, there was a war for independence from South Africa. In Mozambique, the government fought a South African sponsored uprising. In Angola, South African backed rebels fought against the Soviet-backed government and its Cuban allies.

Towards the end of the 1980s, the thaw in the Cold War helped peace agreements emerge. Namibia gained independence and foreign forces withdrew from Angola. At the start of the 1990s, both Angola and Mozambique achieved peace agreements. Though the Angolan agreement did not last, the agreement in Mozambique did, and by 1994 the apartheid system in South Africa had also been peacefully ended.

The end of war in Mozambique released thousands of small arms into circulation in the region, but though there are 400 murders everyday in South Africa, numbers have not increased in the way many feared in the mid-1990s. Millions of South Africans still live in poverty and the end of apartheid has by no means meant the end of inequality: the richest 10 percent of the population earns 40 times as much as the poorest 10 percent.

Mozambique has had even more difficulty in achieving an economic dividend of peace, partly because of its much lower starting point, partly because of the infestation of landmines throughout the country, and partly because of the cyclones and floods that devastated large areas in 2000 and 2001. Some of the flood-hit areas in central Mozambique then suffered drought in 2002.

In Angola, the possibility of peace was dashed when the rebel leader Jonas Savimbi rejected the unfavorable election result in 1992. War continued for another decade until Savimbi's death in early 2002, at which point his UNITA movement sued for peace.

The enemy to peace in South Africa now is the HIV/AIDS epidemic. Medical services are incapable of coping with an ever growing number of infections that was underestimated for much of the 1990s. In 2001, 725,000 people died of AIDS and throughout the region there are now more than 1.7 million children who have been orphaned by AIDS.

## South Africa
Murders with firearms
1994–2000

total murder

murder with firearm

10 854
2000

12 011
1999

12 298
1998

11 224
1997

11 394
1996

11 056
1995

11 134
1994

## HIV/AIDS

number of adults living with HIV/AIDS

number of children living with HIV/AIDS

AIDS deaths *2001*

AIDS orphans

infection rate

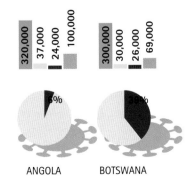

320,000   37,000   24,000   100,000

300,000   30,000   26,000   69,000

6%   36%

ANGOLA        BOTSWANA

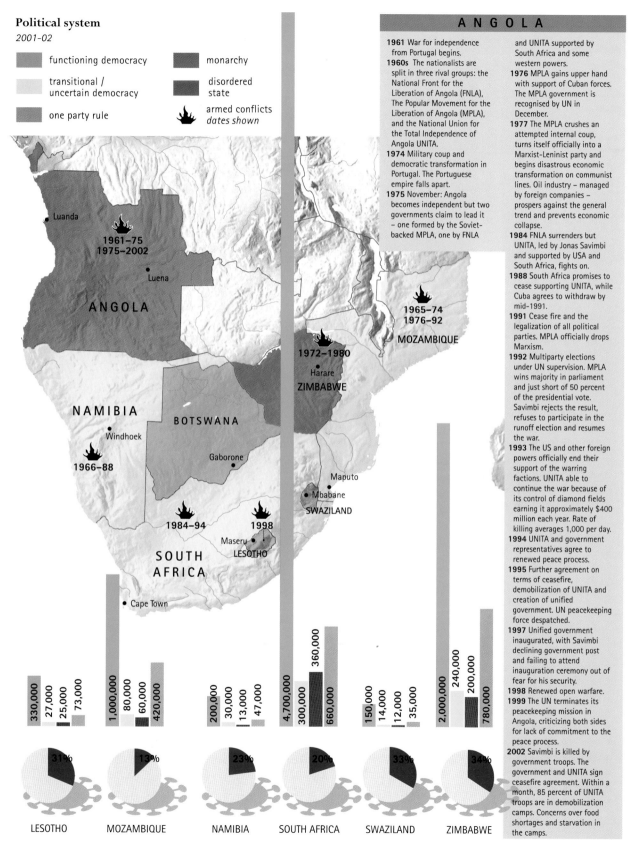

## Political system
*2001-02*

- functioning democracy
- transitional / uncertain democracy
- one party rule
- monarchy
- disordered state
- armed conflicts *dates shown*

Luanda

1961–75
1975–2002

Luena

ANGOLA

NAMIBIA

Windhoek

1966–88

BOTSWANA

Gaborone

1984–94      1998

Maseru
LESOTHO

SOUTH
AFRICA

Cape Town

1972–1980

Harare
ZIMBABWE

1965–74
1976–92

MOZAMBIQUE

Maputo

Mbabane
SWAZILAND

---

### A N G O L A

**1961** War for independence from Portugal begins.

**1960s** The nationalists are split in three rival groups: the National Front for the Liberation of Angola (FNLA), The Popular Movement for the Liberation of Angola (MPLA), and the National Union for the Total Independence of Angola UNITA.

**1974** Military coup and democratic transformation in Portugal. The Portuguese empire falls apart.

**1975** November: Angola becomes independent but two governments claim to lead it – one formed by the Soviet-backed MPLA, one by FNLA and UNITA supported by South Africa and some western powers.

**1976** MPLA gains upper hand with support of Cuban forces. The MPLA government is recognised by UN in December.

**1977** The MPLA crushes an attempted internal coup, turns itself officially into a Marxist-Leninist party and begins disastrous economic transformation on communist lines. Oil industry – managed by foreign companies – prospers against the general trend and prevents economic collapse.

**1984** FNLA surrenders but UNITA, led by Jonas Savimbi and supported by USA and South Africa, fights on.

**1988** South Africa promises to cease supporting UNITA, while Cuba agrees to withdraw by mid-1991.

**1991** Cease fire and the legalization of all political parties. MPLA officially drops Marxism.

**1992** Multiparty elections under UN supervision. MPLA wins majority in parliament and just short of 50 percent of the presidential vote. Savimbi rejects the result, refuses to participate in the runoff election and resumes the war.

**1993** The US and other foreign powers officially end their support of the warring factions. UNITA able to continue the war because of its control of diamond fields earning it approximately $400 million each year. Rate of killing averages 1,000 per day.

**1994** UNITA and government representatives agree to renewed peace process.

**1995** Further agreement on terms of ceasefire, demobilization of UNITA and creation of unified government. UN peacekeeping force despatched.

**1997** Unified government inaugurated, with Savimbi declining government post and failing to attend inauguration ceremony out of fear for his security.

**1998** Renewed open warfare.

**1999** The UN terminates its peacekeeping mission in Angola, criticizing both sides for lack of commitment to the peace process.

**2002** Savimbi is killed by government troops. The government and UNITA sign ceasefire agreement. Within a month, 85 percent of UNITA troops are in demobilization camps. Concerns over food shortages and starvation in the camps.

---

330,000  27,000  25,000  73,000

1,000,000  80,000  60,000  420,000

200,000  30,000  13,000  47,000

4,700,000  300,000  360,000  660,000

150,000  14,000  12,000  35,000

2,000,000  240,000  200,000  780,000

31%    13%    23%    20%    33%    34%

LESOTHO    MOZAMBIQUE    NAMIBIA    SOUTH AFRICA    SWAZILAND    ZIMBABWE

# CHAPTER EIGHT

# Latin America

At the beginning of the 1990s, there were civil wars in Colombia, El Salvador, Guatemala, Nicaragua, Peru and Suriname. At the start of the 21st century, there was civil war only in Colombia.

Alongside the trend away from armed conflict, the democratic trend that began in the 1980s was continued. Argentina, Brazil, Chile and Uruguay all developed an extended experience of democracy. The human rights record in Latin America was better in the 1990s than in the 1980s and before.

In most countries, the long-term causes of conflict and dictatorship persist: there are major inequalities in ownership of land in rural areas, and overwhelming poverty in the large cities. But when a threat of destabilization emerged during 2001 and 2002, its sources did not lie in the traditional patterns and causes of armed conflicts in Latin America. Rather, the problem lay in the modern financial sector.

In late 2001 and into early 2002, Argentina's banking system lay in ruins with economic meltdown imminent. A succession of presidents survived hardly a few days in office. Massive street protests aimed at the incompetence of Argentina's leaders, were peopled mainly by the middle classes, whose lives had been thrown into turmoil by the economic crisis. In March 2002, the value of Venezuela's currency was in free fall and, as in Argentina, the middle classes took to the streets in protest. In Venezuela, the protests were prelude to a military coup in April. The ouster of President Chavez (himself a coup maker ten years before) was quickly reversed, and the degree of popular support for Chavez matched the degree of popular opposition. Further crises followed in Uruguay, where banks were briefly closed and shops looted during protests in the capital, and in Brazil, which received a loan of $30 billion from the International Monetary Fund after an abrupt fall in the value of its currency and its government bonds.

The danger of a succession of such crises is twofold. First, they undermine confidence in the future and build scepticism about the competence and honesty of elected politicians. In political systems with a long tradition – even if not a live one – of strong leaders who either destroyed democracy or more subtly restricted and manipulated it, economic crisis tempts many voters into thinking that all votes are a waste of time. Second, in major economic crises, the richest do not suffer as much as the poorest, but their interests are nonetheless damaged and they not only complain more loudly than the poorest, but have the means to do something about it. The combination of large numbers of people alienated from politics with the determination of a small elite to protect its interests at all costs is a recipe for reversing the combined trend to peace and freedom.

Looming over Latin America is the economic, political and strategic power of the USA. In 1823, President Monroe warned European states against interfering with the newly independent states that were just breaking free from the Spanish empire. Eighty years later, President Theodore Roosevelt introduced a corollary to the Monroe doctrine, asserting a US right to intervene wherever there was misconduct by a Latin American state. The straightforward use of US forces to assert US power declined after the 1920s; with some exceptions the preferred instruments of power were clandestine operations, military assistance to guerrillas or governments, and economic leverage. A modified version of the Roosevelt corollary to the Monroe doctrine was evident in the policies of President Reagan in the 1980s as his government supported conservative regimes and opposed radical ones in Central America and the Caribbean.

The question now is not whether the USA will use its power in Latin America; using power is what great powers do and it is unrealistic to expect otherwise. Rather, the question is for what ends and in what ways it will use its power. Will it seek ways to prevent economic crisis from leading to political instability and violent conflict? Will it try to strengthen the independent political life of Latin American countries? This, after all, is what it tries to do in some of the world's conflict zones. Or will it take sides and concentrate on correcting "misconduct" – as it does in others of the world's conflict zones?

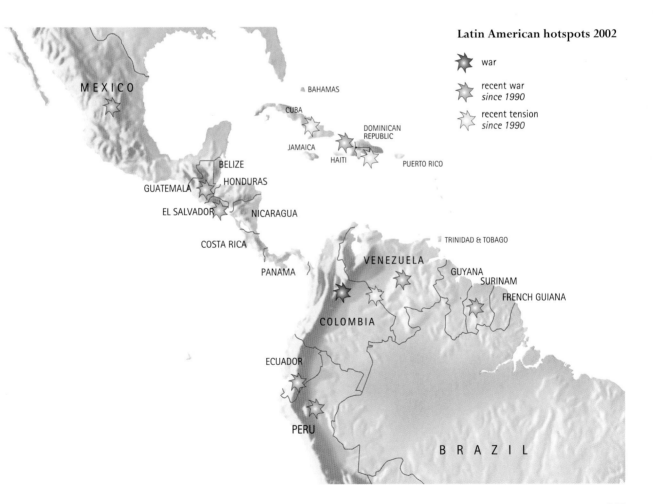

**Latin American hotspots 2002**

⬟ war

⬟ recent war
*since 1990*

⬟ recent tension
*since 1990*

# 40 Colombia and Its Neighbors

Disputes over land and power are behind most of the armed conflicts that have wracked Colombia and the rest of northern South America since independence almost two centuries ago.

Since independence, the states of the region have struggled to fulfil the basic functions of a modern state – unable at home to maintain order, and unable internationally to put national interests ahead of the preferences of their powerful near-neighbor to the north. And for long periods some of the states – especially Bolivia, Ecuador and Venezuela – were ruled by individuals and cliques who showed less interest in the welfare of the country's citizens than in their own enrichment.

In Colombia the causes of each round of war can be traced to the unresolved problems left behind by the previous war. By the time of the 1940s and the 1950s, and the civil war called *La Violencia*, it was almost impossible to trace ideological differences between the protagonists. As peace failed to deliver prosperity in the 1960s, some of the new guerrilla groups, most notably the Colombian Revolutionary Armed Forces (FARC), which remains the most powerful of them some 40 years later, emerged out of community forces that had been formed during *La Violencia*.

Where the coca leaf grows, it offers poor peasants a more profitable crop than most alternatives. It also fuels criminality, and profits from the cocaine trade allow guerrilla groups to arm themselves as well as any national army in the region – for most of the 1990s, FARC had more fighters in the field than the Colombian army. The combination of persistent war and powerful criminal organizations in Colombia is a threat to the region as fighting spills over into neighboring states, cocaine corruption burrows into them, and refugees cross borders needing help and protection.

## Coca leaf production
thousand tonnes

Bolivia:77
Colombia:45
Peru:198
Colombia:195
Bolivia:23
Peru:69

**1990**     **1999**

Bolivia, Colombia and Peru produce between them almost the whole world's supply of cocaine. Effective anti-narcotic programmes in Bolivia and Peru have reduced the total coca leaf harvest but accelerated expansion in Colombia. Colombia is also the world's fourth largest producer of opium.

## Colombian cocaine exports

USA
EUROPE
MEXICO
CARIBBEAN
NIGERIA
COLOMBIA
BRAZIL
SOUTH AFRICA

→ Main identified cocaine routes

## Colombia

**1821** Independence as Gran Colombia, including modern day Ecuador, Panama, and Venezuela.
**1829–30** Secession of Ecuador and Venezuela.
**1840** Civil war interrupts industrialization and disrupts trade.
**late 1840s** Delineation of rival groups into Liberal (modern, trade-oriented) and Conservative (traditional, landed interests) parties.
**1860s–1870s** "Epoch of Civil Wars": collapse of public order.
**1880s** Further civil conflict.
**1899–1903** "War of a Thousand Days" between Liberals and Conservatives: 60,000 – 130,000 deaths.
**1903** Treaty with US for a canal in Panama rejected by Colombian Senate. Panamanian rebellion, discreetly aided by US, and secession.
**1946–64** "*La Violencia*": over 200,000 deaths in Liberal-Conservative conflict (some estimates up to 350,000).
**1953 and 1957** Military coups.
**1957** Power sharing agreement between Liberals and Conservatives (rotating presidency, 50/50 representation in government and legislature.
**early 1960s** Economic stagnation and hyper-inflation.
**1964** Formation of National Liberation Army (ELN).
**1966** Formation of Colombian Revolutionary Armed Forces (FARC).
**1973–74** Formation of 19th of April Movement (M-19).
**late 1970s** Major expansion of narcotic production and exports from Colombia – first marijuana, then cocaine.
**1985** M-19 seizure of hundreds of hostages in Palace of Justice, leading to military assault killing 100 including half the Supreme Court judges.
**1980s** Para-military groups formed by landowners to fight leftist guerrillas; growth in drug trade and rise of the Medellin and Cali cocaine cartels.
**1989** M-19's transformation into legal political party following peace agreement with government.
**1991–92** Government negotiations with ELN and FARC.
**1998** Renewed negotiations with ELN and FARC. Granting to FARC of safe enclave (approximately the size of Switzerland) to encourage participation in peace process.
**2000** US military assistance costing $1 billion to fight cocaine trade.
**2002** Peace negotiations ended. FARC warning to over 100 mayors to quit their posts or be killed.

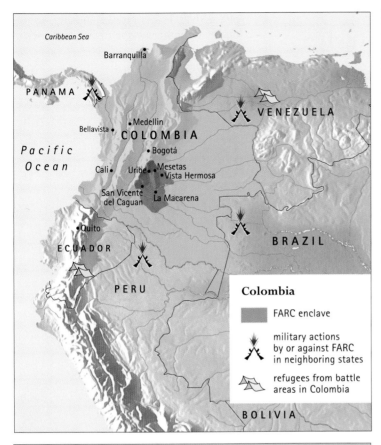

Caribbean Sea

PANAMA

Barranquilla

Bellavista • Medellín
COLOMBIA

Pacific Ocean

Cali • Uribe • Mesetas
• Bogotá
Vista Hermosa
San Vicente • La Macarena
del Caguan

• Quito

ECUADOR

PERU

VENEZUELA

BRAZIL

BOLIVIA

**Colombia**

█ FARC enclave

⚔ military actions by or against FARC in neighboring states

⛺ refugees from battle areas in Colombia

## Venezuela

**1830** Secession from Gran Colombia.
**1830–1945** Rule by succession of *caudillos* (military strongmen).
**pre-1914** Initial exploitation of oil resources.
**1920s** World's leading exporter of oil.
**1945–48** Combined military and civilian coup establishing first Venezuelan government backed by majority of people under President Betancourt.
**1948–58** Military dictatorship.
**1959** Romulo Betancourt elected President for 2nd (and in 1963 for 3rd) term.
**1969** First case in Venezuela of a president leaving office because of election results.
**1970s–1980s** Economic boom based on rising world oil price rises, followed by recession caused by fall in oil prices.
**1989** Riots over austerity measures, widespread looting, hundreds killed.
**1992** Attempted coup led by Colonel Hugo Chavez.
**1998** Chavez elected President (re-elected 2000).
**2001** Millions in rallies against government's economic policies.
**2002** Failed coup attempt against President Chavez.

## Bolivia

**1825** Independence.
**1825–80** Domination of politics and government by *caudillos* (military strongmen, governing autocratically and for private gain).
**1879–83** War with Chile. Loss of coastal region.
**1880** Era of civilian government begins.
**1932–35** The "Chaco War" with Paraguay: Defeat at cost of 57,000 lives lost and territory ceded.
**1936** Military coup: further coups and uprisings 1943, 1946, 1951.
**1952** Uprising: reforming civilian governments till 1964.
**1964–78** Military dictatorship under successive leaders.
**1978–79** Attempt to return to civilian rule.
**1980** The "Cocaine coup" bringing General Meza to power: extreme repression, widespread murders, torture, corruption, coup leaders' involvement in cocaine trafficking.
**1981** Return to civilian rule.
**late 1980s** US military assistance to Bolivian government in war on drug trade.

## Ecuador

**1830** Secession from Gran Colombia.
**1830–1925** Politics dominated by rivalry between Liberals (business interests) and Conservative (landed interests); both kinds of government tending equally to authoritarianism.
**1925** Military coup: no end to political authoritarianism, turbulence, and economic weakness.
**1948–60** Period of constitutional government and economic growth.
**1963–66** Military dictatorship.
**1972–79** Military dictatorship.
**1979** Return to civilian government.
**1987** President Cordero kidnapped and beaten up by the army in protest at his economic policies.
**2000** President Mahaud forced out by army coup backed by mass protests.

## Peru

**1824** Peru gains independence.
**1968–78** Military dictatorship.
**1980** Uprising by "*Sendero Luminoso*" ("Shining Path") guerrillas.
**1980–85** Inflation rate rises to 3,240 percent.
**1990** Election of Alberto Fujimori as President. Introduction of economic austerity measures including 3,000 percent increase in price of petrol, causing prices of all basic goods to rise.
**1992** Fujimori's "self-administered coup", dissolving Congress and suspending constitution with military help. *Sendero* leader captured.
**1993** New constitution promulgated to permit Fujimori to stand for re-election.
**1994** 6,000 *Sendero* guerrillas surrender.
**2000** Administration hit by bribery scandals, Fujimori's resignation and subsequent flight to Japan.
**2001** Arrest warrant issued for Fujimori.
**2002** Violent protests and evidence of renewed activity by *Sendero* (probably numbering approximately 400 guerrillas).

# 41 | Central America

The countries of Central America have been even less successful than their larger southern neighbours in finding internal harmony and have been even more subject to the preferences and policies of the USA.

### The Guatemalan peace process
Over 200,000 people were killed in the civil war. The military openly used massacre as a tactic of terror. Against this background, in 1987 came the first contacts between government and rebels. Three years later, in Oslo, agreement was reached on establishing a peace process. Meanwhile, war continued and after Oslo the peace process seemed to have stalled. Then in January 1994 came a framework agreement to resume negotiations, with the support of a "Group of Friends" consisting of Colombia, Mexico, Norway, Spain, the USA and Venezuela. There followed successive agreements on:
- a timetable for the process, human rights, resettlement of displaced population groups, and a truth commission (all in March 1994);
- the rights of indigenous peoples (March 1995);
- socio-economic aspects (May 1996);
- reduced role of armed forces (September 1996);
- ceasefire, constitutional reforms, legalisation of rebel organisation, law on national reconciliation, procedure for implementing and monitoring compliance, and the final peace accord (all in December 1996).

The Guatemalan peace process is unusual in being so comprehensive, especially in its inclusion of socio-economic problems as part of the peace deal. This reflected the aim of dealing with the underlying causes of the war.

Implementation of this complex series of agreements was to have been completed by the end of 2000. This was too ambitious: implementation was patchy. It was particularly slow in relation to indigenous rights. And while 93 percent of atrocities

### The Soccer War

In 1969, three hard fought qualifying games between El Salvador and Honduras for the following year's World Cup were the prelude to a war between the two countries. Its causes lay in a long-standing border dispute, and in resentment in Honduras about the large number of Salvadoran migrants in the country. The Honduran government introduced a policy of forced repatriation. Reports circulated of mistreatment of the Salvadoran migrants and the government of Salvador opened hostilities. The war lasted two weeks, cost several thousand lives, and was not formally settled by treaty until 1980.

## Guatemala

**1823** Inclusion in United Provinces of Central America.
**1838** Independent statehood.
**1944** Dictatorship overthrown by popular uprising, new democratic constitution introduced.
**1951** Jacobo Arbenz elected President, radical land reform initiated threatening US interests, especially United Fruit Company.
**1954** Arbenz ousted in uprising organised by CIA, opening prolonged period of political instability.
**1968** Start of civil war.
**1996** Final Peace Accord: end of civil war.

## El Salvador

**1824** Inclusion in Federal Republic of Central America.
**1841** Independent statehood.
**1931** Military coup initiates succession of military-dominated governments, supported by landed elite.
**1932** Farm workers uprising suppressed with execution of over 10,000 suspected participants.
**1969** "Soccer War" with Honduras.
**1970s** Increase in mass opposition to regime, and in repression. Growing elite disenchantment with military rule.
**1979** Start of open civil war.
**1980** Collapse of military government, start of effort to bring in civilian rule; throughout 1980s, international observers deeply sceptical of fairness of successive elections.
**1981** Financial assistance and military training from USA in war against leftist guerrillas.
**1991** War ends by agreement.

## Honduras

**1823** Inclusion in United Provinces of Central America.
**1838** Independent statehood.
**1963–71** and **1972–81** Military dictatorship.
**1969** "Soccer War" with El Salvador.
**1980s** Base for US-supported Contras attempting to overthrow left-wing Sandinistas in Nicaragua.
**1998** Hurricane Mitch: several thousand dead; over a million people forced from their homes; widespread destruction of roads, towns and farm areas.

carried out during the war were committed by the government side, there has been little action to bring those responsible to account. In 1999, the constitutional reforms agreed in the peace process were turned down in a referendum with a very low turn out (less than 19 percent of those eligible to vote). Peace remained fragile.

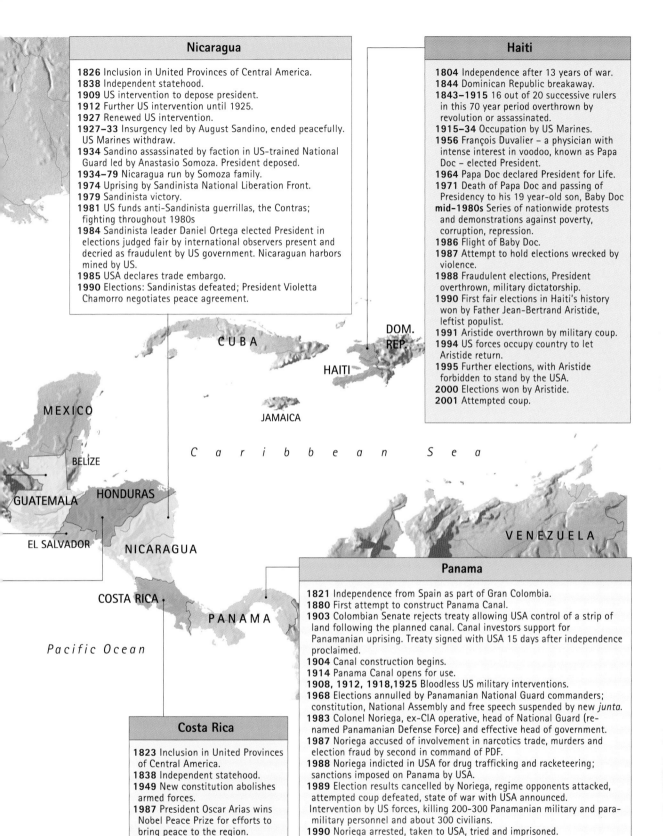

## Nicaragua

**1826** Inclusion in United Provinces of Central America.
**1838** Independent statehood.
**1909** US intervention to depose president.
**1912** Further US intervention until 1925.
**1927** Renewed US intervention.
**1927–33** Insurgency led by August Sandino, ended peacefully. US Marines withdraw.
**1934** Sandino assassinated by faction in US-trained National Guard led by Anastasio Somoza. President deposed.
**1934–79** Nicaragua run by Somoza family.
**1974** Uprising by Sandinista National Liberation Front.
**1979** Sandinista victory.
**1981** US funds anti-Sandinista guerrillas, the Contras; fighting throughout 1980s
**1984** Sandinista leader Daniel Ortega elected President in elections judged fair by international observers present and decried as fraudulent by US government. Nicaraguan harbors mined by US.
**1985** USA declares trade embargo.
**1990** Elections: Sandinistas defeated; President Violetta Chamorro negotiates peace agreement.

## Haiti

**1804** Independence after 13 years of war.
**1844** Dominican Republic breakaway.
**1843–1915** 16 out of 20 successive rulers in this 70 year period overthrown by revolution or assassinated.
**1915–34** Occupation by US Marines.
**1956** François Duvalier – a physician with intense interest in voodoo, known as Papa Doc – elected President.
**1964** Papa Doc declared President for Life.
**1971** Death of Papa Doc and passing of Presidency to his 19 year-old son, Baby Doc
**mid-1980s** Series of nationwide protests and demonstrations against poverty, corruption, repression.
**1986** Flight of Baby Doc.
**1987** Attempt to hold elections wrecked by violence.
**1988** Fraudulent elections, President overthrown, military dictatorship.
**1990** First fair elections in Haiti's history won by Father Jean-Bertrand Aristide, leftist populist.
**1991** Aristide overthrown by military coup.
**1994** US forces occupy country to let Aristide return.
**1995** Further elections, with Aristide forbidden to stand by the USA.
**2000** Elections won by Aristide.
**2001** Attempted coup.

CUBA

DOM. REP.

HAITI

JAMAICA

*Caribbean Sea*

MEXICO

BELIZE

GUATEMALA

HONDURAS

EL SALVADOR

NICARAGUA

VENEZUELA

COSTA RICA

PANAMA

*Pacific Ocean*

## Panama

**1821** Independence from Spain as part of Gran Colombia.
**1880** First attempt to construct Panama Canal.
**1903** Colombian Senate rejects treaty allowing USA control of a strip of land following the planned canal. Canal investors support for Panamanian uprising. Treaty signed with USA 15 days after independence proclaimed.
**1904** Canal construction begins.
**1914** Panama Canal opens for use.
**1908, 1912, 1918,1925** Bloodless US military interventions.
**1968** Elections annulled by Panamanian National Guard commanders; constitution, National Assembly and free speech suspended by new *junta*.
**1983** Colonel Noriega, ex-CIA operative, head of National Guard (re-named Panamanian Defense Force) and effective head of government.
**1987** Noriega accused of involvement in narcotics trade, murders and election fraud by second in command of PDF.
**1988** Noriega indicted in USA for drug trafficking and racketeering; sanctions imposed on Panama by USA.
**1989** Election results cancelled by Noriega, regime opponents attacked, attempted coup defeated, state of war with USA announced. Intervention by US forces, killing 200-300 Panamanian military and para-military personnel and about 300 civilians.
**1990** Noriega arrested, taken to USA, tried and imprisoned.

## Costa Rica

**1823** Inclusion in United Provinces of Central America.
**1838** Independent statehood.
**1949** New constitution abolishes armed forces.
**1987** President Oscar Arias wins Nobel Peace Prize for efforts to bring peace to the region.

# CHAPTER NINE

# Peacebuilding

**POLITICAL FRAMEWORK**

**Democratization:**
organizing and monitoring elections

**Human Rights:**
respect for international law, development of monitoring and reporting of abuses

**Rule of law:**
improving the drafting of laws, judicial reform, police reform

**Good governance:**
transparency, accountability, anti-corruption

**Building political institutions**

FIFTY FOUR PERCENT OF PEACE AGREEMENTS break down within five years of signature. Experience in the 1990s suggests they generally break down for one or more of five main reasons:

• One party (and sometimes both) is insincere: they lie and cheat and their signature on the agreement is a fraud; perhaps surprisingly, straightforward dishonesty of this kind is rather rare. The RUF rebel force in Sierra Leone was a clear example of a party that signed agreements with no honest commitment to them.

• The commitment of one party (and sometimes both) to the agreement was conditional in ways that it did not make clear until too late. For example, when Jonas Savimbi did not win the election in Angola in 1992, the whole point of the peace process so far as he was concerned was no longer valid. So he pulled out and returned the country to a further decade of war.

• One party (and sometimes both) fragmented, often as a direct result of the agreement. Internal divisions are often a more important determinant of peace and war than divisions between the two parties. Israel/Palestine is an example of a peace process made unworkable by internal divisions on both sides; Northern Ireland is an example of a peace process that survived several crises caused by internal divisions on first one side, then the other.

• The consequences of the war – economic, military, human, political and/or social – are so heavy that the country cannot function normally. Peace does not fulfil its promise, and the dashing of hopes forms the breeding ground for disillusion and a willingness to return to violence. The experience of war does not always warn people to avoid war. Many people respond to war by having greater inhibitions against the use of violence, but at least as many respond with a greater willingness for violence.

• The long-term causes of the original war are not addressed and the problems not solved, and after a while the country slides back into war because there is nowhere else for it to go and no leader knows how to do anything else.

In 1992, the then UN Secretary-General Boutros Boutros Ghali wrote a report for the Security Council in which he distinguished between different kinds of peace operations. Peacekeeping happens when an agreement has been reached, peace enforcement is what may happen if the Security Council decides to impose peace on a conflict region, and preventive diplomacy is an intervention in a high-risk region to stop conflict escalating into war. Peacebuilding is the

**RECONCILIATION**

**Dialogue:**
between political leaders, among political activists, NGOs

**Building mutual understanding:**
work on education curricula, especially history

**Avoidance of hate speech and hostile rhetoric:**
standards for the news media

**Truth commissions**

name Boutros Ghali gave to the process of trying to help a society recover from conflict. It is more than post-war reconstruction – for to reconstruct after a war may simply be to put back in place the systems and structures that led to war in the first place.

Peacebuilding is complex, expensive and slow. Its four components – security, socio-economic development, building political institutions and reconciliation - are like interdependent pillars; if one is weak, the whole structure may collapse.

The peacebuilders – the UN, other inter-governmental organizations, international non-governmental organizations – are the custodians of peace and must prevent spoilers from sabotaging the peace process. The custodians have to end war-time black markets and the accompanying corruption so that ordinary economic functioning can start. They have to clear the landmines so rural life can resume, turn fighters into workers and consumers, deal with traumatized child soldiers, and encourage reconciliation between groups who are committed to the language of mutual hatred. Through all this, they will be criticized from inside the country for acting like latter day colonialists, and from outside the country for not doing enough quickly enough. And despite the scale of the effort, and the breadth and depth of the activities they take on, they must also understand that, as custodians, they are only there to offer help and encouragement, for the real sources of long-term peace lie within the war-torn country.

Compared to the four-pillared structure, some of the major peacebuilding efforts of the 1990s looked more like a three-legged stool: a major security force, heaps of money and elections as quick as possible. In most cases it is not that easy and it is counter-productive to act as if it were.

The intertwined difficulties of recovering from war are often hard to understand for those who have lived all their lives in peaceful conditions. Life under war-time pressure – such as being forced to flee your home and live in a refugee camp, or being forced to stay in your home in the siege of Sarajevo from 1992 to 1995 – can make it hard to think much about the future beyond a very few days. How can you make plans for next year if you or someone you love might be shot on the way to get bread tomorrow?

But if you lose the ability to think about next year, how can you make plans for your education, or to open a business committing yourself to hard work in the expectation of the profits flowing in next year? And if people cannot think about training, education or investment, there is no way towards economic recovery; there is only dependence on external aid until international funding agencies become disillusioned or decide to concentrate on another conflict.

Political leaders are often impatient with the peacebuilding efforts they support. They tend to show even less interest in supporting similar efforts in order to prevent a war from breaking out – for no politician ever got re-elected by preventing wars that might not have happened in countries no voter ever heard of.

And yet, in spite of all this, after the first decade of peacebuilding, governments, inter-governmental organizations and international non-governmental organizations are developing experience, working out what to do and what not to do. There continue to be failures; there are also some successes.

**SECURITY**

Securing peace, monitoring ceasefire etc

Disarmament, demobilization and reintegration of combatants in ordinary society

Care for child soldiers

Humanitarian mine clearance

Security sector reform

Controls on the trade in small arms and light weapons

**SOCIO-ECONOMIC**

Physical reconstruction

Investment in utilities and economic infra-structure

Anti-corruption laws

Schools

Hospitals

Return of refugees

# 42 Peace Agreements

1994 1998
UNITED KINGDOM

199
SLOVEN

FRANCE

SPAIN

1992 1995
CROATIA

19
19
BOS
HERZE

MOROCCO

ALGERIA

LIE

WESTERN
SAHARA

MAURITANIA

1995
MALI

NIGER

197

SENEGAL

1991

GUINEA-
BISSAU    GUINEA

CÔTE d'
IVOIRE

GHANA
TOGO

NIGERIA

2002 1999
SIERRA LEONE

LIBERIA

1997

1999
1994
CONGO

2002 19
ANG

NA

USA

1995
MEXICO

1996
GUATEMALA

HAITI

EL SALVADOR

1990
NICARAGUA

1991

VENEZUELA

TRINIDAD & TOBAGO

SURINAME

1992

1998
COLOMBIA

ECUADOR

1995
PERU

Armed conflicts end in other ways than by agreement – through victory and defeat, through the exhaustion of one side or both, through a fundamental change in the circumstances that started the conflict. When peace agreements are reached, that may only be the end of the beginning of what will turn out to be a long process, in which failure will often seem the most likely outcome and the threat of disaster is ever present. As the years go by in this difficult and fragile process, both sides may become more and more committed to the process, to the point that peace seems inevitable, no longer a goal but a fact of life. Sometimes, however, the passing years seem to blunt the collective memory of the horrors of war, and politicians come to the fore who are willing to take risks with peace. When fighting returns after an agreement has been broken, it is often more violent than before.

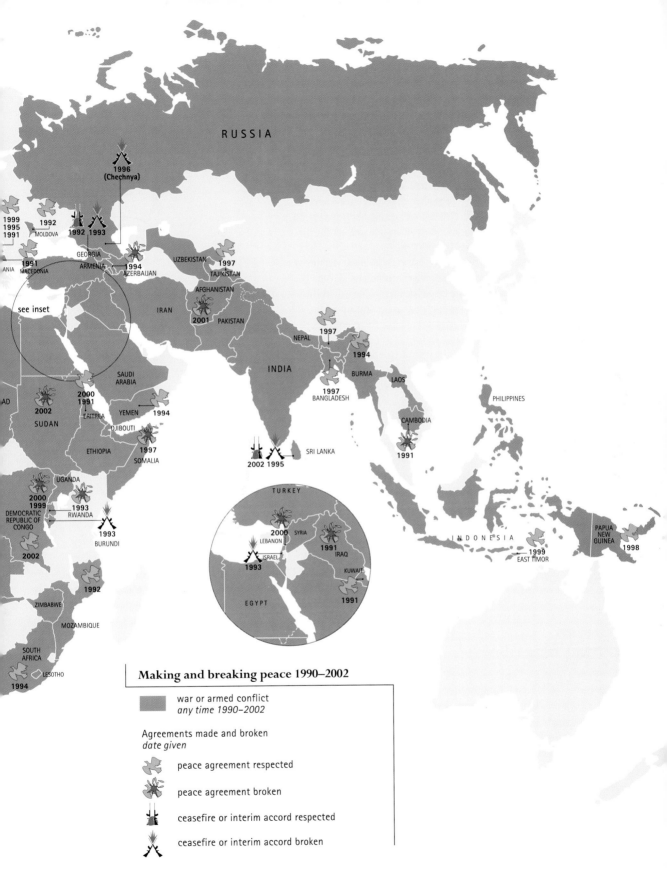

RUSSIA

1996
(Chechnya)

1999
1995
1991

1992
MOLDOVA

1992  1993

ANIA
MACEDONIA

1991

GEORGIA

ARMENIA

1994
AZERBAIJAN

UZBEKISTAN

1997
TAJIKISTAN

AFGHANISTAN

2001  PAKISTAN

IRAN

see inset

SAUDI
ARABIA

2000
1991

ERITREA

YEMEN

1994

AD

2002

SUDAN

DJIBOUTI

ETHIOPIA

1997

SOMALIA

NEPAL

1997

INDIA

BURMA

1994

LAOS

1997
BANGLADESH

PHILIPPINES

CAMBODIA

1991

SRI LANKA

2002  1995

UGANDA

2000
1999

DEMOCRATIC
REPUBLIC OF
CONGO

1993
RWANDA

1993
BURUNDI

2002

1992

ZIMBABWE

MOZAMBIQUE

SOUTH
AFRICA

LESOTHO

1994

INDONESIA

1999
EAST TIMOR

PAPUA
NEW
GUINEA

1998

TURKEY

2000
LEBANON

ISRAEL

1993

SYRIA

1991

IRAQ

KUWAIT

1991

EGYPT

## Making and breaking peace 1990–2002

war or armed conflict
*any time 1990–2002*

Agreements made and broken
*date given*

peace agreement respected

peace agreement broken

ceasefire or interim accord respected

ceasefire or interim accord broken

# 43 | Peacekeeping

## United Nations peacekeeping

### Active missions

*The first UN peacekeeping mission started in 1948. In 2002 there were 15 active UN peacekeeping missions.*

**1950**

**1960**

**1970**

**1980**

**1990**

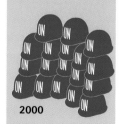

**2000**

The end of the Cold War in 1989 freed the United Nations from the restrictions that superpower rivalry had placed on it. One major consequence was the ability to deploy more peacekeeping operations. Where the first four decades of peacekeeping saw 15 missions, as many were started in the first four years of the 1990s.

Not only were operations more frequent, they were also more ambitious. From monitoring ceasefires and lines of military disengagement, peacekeeping operations expanded into preparing for elections, reintegrating fighters into society, training the police and trying to encourage reconciliation. Inevitably, with such high ambitions, there have been failures.

The tasks that peacekeeping forces are given are often quite out of range of their abilities. The aims expressed in UN Security Council decisions are often not backed in practice by member states and many operations are under-funded and under-staffed.

In most peacekeeping operations, the soldiers are lightly armed and can use force only in self-defense, after they have been fired on. Sending such forces into a war zone under the label of peacekeeping – when there is in fact no peace to keep – led in Bosnia-Herzegovina to the helplessness of Dutch UN peacekeepers as the Bosnian Serb army massacred 7,000 people in Srebrenica in 1995. In Sierra Leone in 2000, insurgent forces trapped and held hostage 500 UN peacekeepers.

In many cases, however – such as in Central America, Mozambique, Namibia, Cambodia – UN peacekeeping missions have helped war-torn societies find their way from an initial agreement on ending the war towards a relatively stable peace that gives them a chance of something better.

**NATO states' contribution to UN and to non-UN peacekeeping operations**
*Dissatisfaction with the UN and its operations in the mid-1990s led to several states, most notably the USA, preferring to place the forces they committed to peacekeeping under a command structure outside the UN. In two of the largest and highest profile operations – Bosnia-Herzegovina since 1995 and Kosovo since 1999 – the military forces are not under the command of the UN mission.*

Ratio between numbers of military personnel committed to non-UN and to UN peacekeeping operations
2001–02

| | | |
|---|---|---|
| | Belgium 75 : 1 | Spain 500 : 1 |
| France, Italy, UK 15 : 1 | Norway 60 : 1 | USA 350 : 1 |
| Poland 0.8 : 1 | Denmark, Hungary 12 : 1 | Germany 30 : 1 | Greece 190 : 1 |
| Portugal 0.7 : 1 | Canada 8 : 1 | Czech Republic 25 : 1 | Turkey 160 : 1 |
| | | Netherlands 130 : 1 |

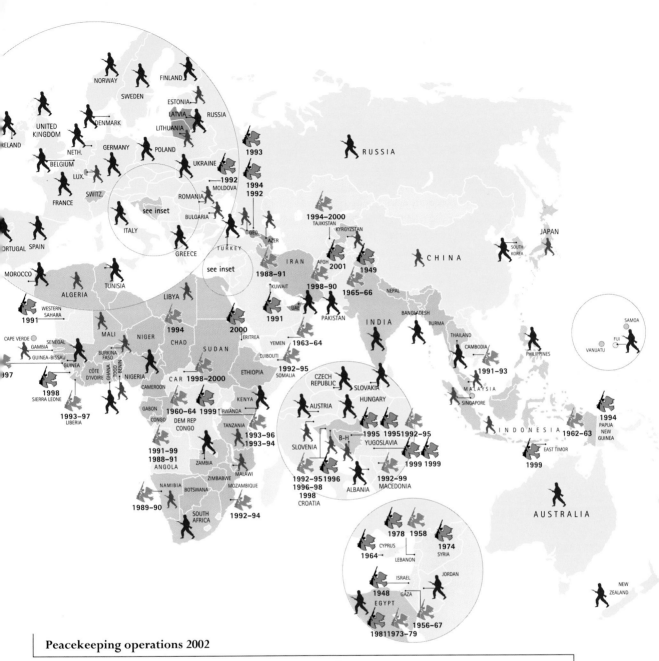

## Peacekeeping operations 2002

States that committed military personnel
and / or police:

- both to UN and to non-UN peacekeeping operations
- only to UN peacekeeping operations
- only to non-UN peacekeeping operations
- other states that committed military or police personnel to earlier UN peacekeeping operations
- other states

over 100 personnel in peacekeeping
operations of all kinds *2002*

less than 100 personnel in peacekeeping
operations of all kinds *2002*

### Locations

location of UN peacekeeping operations,
active 2002
*starting date shown*

location of non-UN peacekeeping operations,
active 2002
*starting date shown*

location of earlier UN peacekeeping operations
*start and finish dates shown*

# 44 Peace Processes

It does not take special qualities in political leaders to start a war, but it takes a special type of leader who can blend vision with pragmatism to lead the way from war to peace. Destruction is easier than reconstruction, and what is needed is often more than simple reconstruction. Not surprisingly, the record of peacebuilding is mixed and the prospects are often hard to read. However dire a country's peace prospects seem at any one moment, it is worth remembering that agreement has been possible even in armed conflicts as long as Northern Ireland's, as brutal as Cambodia's and as deep-seated as South Africa's.

The summaries here reflect conditions in late 2002.

## Kosovo

*Peace prospects: Dependent on continued external support*
NATO's war on Yugoslavia ended with an international force going into Kosovo. Militant Albanian nationalists continued to carry out sporadic acts of violence against Serbs and Albanian political rivals. The October 2002 municipal elections were scarred by violence between political parties. In most Serb municipalities, voter turnout was low, revealing profound scepticism that Kosovo's Albanians want or will accept a multi-ethnic Kosovo. There has been significant economic development but the province remains dependent on external aid, and its constitutional status – to become independent or a part of Serbia, which is its current legal status – remained unclear.
*See pages 54–57*

## Northern Ireland

*Peace prospects: Fair*
The ceasefire in 1994 and the Good Friday Peace Agreement of 1998 brought an end to most violence between the two communities of Northern Ireland, but did not end violence within them. The Unionists remained highly distrustful of the IRA's reluctance to give up its weapons; the Loyalists insisted on maintaining their traditional marches. But both the Dublin and London governments have invested enormous prestige in the peace process, and Northern Ireland has benefited. Although the peace process has limped from one crisis to the next, and remains vulnerable to political irresponsibility, only a tiny minority wants to go back to war.
*See pages 40, 50–51*

## Guatemala

*Peace prospects: Fair*
The peace process that produced the 1996 agreement took over six years. Although the agreement was too ambitious and impatient, and the first six years of implementation barely addressed the underlying causes of the war, it did appear to convince ordinary people not to go back to war. Even in the face of severe economic shortcomings, there was no return to open armed conflict and no evidence that any major group was planning one. Political rivalries continue and the country's prospects depend on political leaders having the responsibility to handle these in a peaceful manner.
*See pages 40, 104–105*

## Sierra Leone

*Peace prospects: 50:50*
Successive deals brokered by the UN and the deployment of the largest UN peacekeeping force could not persuade the rebels of the Revolutionary United Front to bring war to an end. Closely linked with President Taylor in neighboring Liberia, and profiting from the diamond trade, the RUF were classic peace spoilers. In 2000 they took peacekeepers hostage and launched an offensive into the capital Freetown. In a short military intervention, British forces delivered a heavy blow to RUF morale. The RUF leader was captured by the government of Sierra Leone and the hostage crisis ended. Demobilization of the RUF and some of the other militias was under way in 2001, and in 2002 a peace agreement was achieved. Sierra Leone is the world's poorest country with a long way to go before finding a secure peace. If the government can prevent the rise of another force like the RUF, and war does not spill over from neighboring states, the country has a chance.
*See pages 40, 88–89*

## South Africa

*Peace prospects: Solid*
President de Klerk's decision to visit ANC leader Nelson Mandela in prison, and Mandela's decision to talk to him, revealed the highest qualities of political leadership in both men. During the negotiations and the constitutional discussions that followed Mandela's release in 1990, the two remained political rivals, but balanced this with partnership in the peace process. Peace was threatened by violence between black South Africans fighting for shares of post-apartheid power. Like much of southern Africa, the country is reeling from the impact of HIV / AIDS and the gulf between rich and poor is huge. A return to open armed conflict seems unlikely, even though the political giants have left the stage.
*See pages 98–99*

## Bosnia-Herzegovina

*Peace prospects: Dependent on continued external support*
The 1995 Dayton peace agreement between Bosnia-Herzegovina, Croatia and Yugoslavia brought an end to three years of war. An international force has prevented any new fighting. Economic development has been minimal, corruption is widespread and the country is dependent on subsidies from abroad. Bosnia-Herzegovina is a loose union of three components – one Croatian, one Serb and one largely Bosniak. Leading Croatian and Serb politicians in Bosnia-Herzegovina have little commitment to creating a unified, viable country, and they get the wrong kind of encouragement from nationalist parties in Croatia and Serbia. Turnout for elections is low, reflecting widespread disillusion and distrust in politicians. Most fear that if the international force is withdrawn, the ensuing risk of war would be high.
*See pages 40, 52–53, 56–57*

## Chechnya

*Peace prospects: Minimal*
The 1996 peace agreement was little more than a truce. It grew out of Russia's inability to win the war and did not reflect any desire on either side to compromise in the long term. A proper settlement – and a decision on Chechnyan independence – was deferred for five years, but a new war began after only three. Both sides have boxed themselves into non-negotiable corners and on both sides there has been extreme violence. It will take a change of leadership on one or both sides before talks could begin.
*See pages 33, 41, 58–59*

## Sri Lanka

*Peace prospects: 50:50*
In 2002 against most people's expectations the government and the Tamil Tigers not only produced a ceasefire agreement with Norwegian mediation, but also sat down for peace talks and started to negotiate seriously. If the Sri Lankan government can agree to formalize Tamil autonomy, and if the Tigers stop pressing for total independence, an agreement is within reach despite the bitterness of the war. Disunity in the Sri Lankan government (President from one party, Prime Minister and parliamentary majority from another) is one reason why the peace process may be destabilized.
*See pages 80–81*

## Cambodia

*Peace prospects: Solid*
The 1992 peace agreement ended Southeast Asia's most vicious war not because all parties agreed to it, but because enough parties agreed to it that the Khmer Rouge finally became irrelevant even in its own eyes. When the Khmer Rouge was unable to stop the first elections, despite killing election monitors and shelling voters on their way to the polling stations, its demise was inevitable.
*See pages 41, 82*

## Iraq

*Peace prospects: Uncertain*
As war against Iraq was planned in 2002, more US attention was given to how it would be fought than to what would follow. There is the problem of building stable political institutions in a country with no democracy, which has been ruled by a state whose principle instrument of control is fear. The unity of the country is also questionable because Iraq's population includes a large minority of Kurds, whose leaders seek autonomy – an arrangement that would not be welcomed in neighboring Turkey for fear it would encourage a return to militancy among some Turkish Kurds. At least Iraq has massive oil reserves with which to finance development. As its neighbors show, however, oil wealth is no guarantee of peace.
*See pages 41, 62–63, 70–77*

## Mozambique

*Peace prospects: Solid*
Of all peace processes, perhaps the most unlikely, though the Renamo guerrillas were clearly going to be left without their regional backers once South Africa began going through its own transformation. Few believed the Renamo insurgent force would transform itself into a political party, and even fewer thought it would respect an unfavorable election result. Encouraged by the UN, however, it took on the role of parliamentary opposition party, and as a result the country was able to leave behind decades of war.
*See pages 98–99*

## Israel and Palestine

*Peace prospects: Dire*
The Oslo process deliberately deferred the difficult questions and tried to secure agreement on those issues where agreement was possible. But in less than three years the peace process was dying. It was finally killed in 2000, when negotiations revealed the gulf between what the two sides consider a reasonable arrangement in the shared city of Jerusalem, and the start of the second intifada buried it. Extremes of violence on both sides and mutual distrust have made it hard to see how agreement could be reached.
*See pages 41, 64–67*

# Table of Wars

The definition used to compile this list of wars and in preparing the maps in this atlas recognizes events as wars or armed conflicts when they entail all of the following:
• open armed conflict
• at least two parties
• centrally organized fighters and fighting
• contestation over political power and/or the control of territory
• continuity between clashes
• a minimum of 25 battle deaths in a 12-month period in the context of a total death toll of at least several hundred.

Unlike some researchers, this definition makes no distinction between the two terms "war" and "armed conflicts"; they are used interchangeably throughout.

The annual threshold of 25 deaths seems very low to many people, but is necessary because the pattern of combat in many of today's wars involves long periods of relative inaction and sudden spurts of extreme violence. A higher threshold would misleadingly suggest that these wars are very brief, when in fact they are often of very long duration.

Even so, there are wars in which activity is either completely terminated or at such a low level it is below the threshold, but then return. Because of this, the table does not refer to wars as ended or terminated, but as suspended.

One feature missing from the definition is the word "state". Until recently it would have been the norm to record events as war or armed conflict only if they involved a state on at least one side, but when events take place that are exactly the same as war except that neither of the parties is recognized as a state by the United Nations, declaring those events not to be war seems purely arbitrary and misleading. Wars without states have occurred in Somalia, Somaliland, northern Iraq and in places such as Lebanon or Liberia where the state has collapsed and there is no effective state power for a period.

The table records the status of wars in November 2002.

# Table of Wars 1990–2002

| Countries | Type of war | Site of war |
|---|---|---|
| Afghanistan | civil war | general |
| Albania | civil war | southern regions |
| Algeria | civil war | general |
| Angola | civil war | general |
| | regional civil war | Cabinda enclave |
| | intervention in DR Congo | DR Congo |
| Armenia | interstate war | Nagorno Karabakh and border region with Azerbaijan |
| Azerbaijan | interstate war | Nagorno Karabakh and border region with Armenia |
| Bangladesh | regional civil war | Chittagong Hill Tracts |
| Bosnia-Herzegovina | civil war | general |
| | regional civil war | central regions |
| Burma | regional civil war | Kachin |
| | regional civil war | Shan |
| | regional civil war | Karen |
| | civil war | general |
| | regional civil war | Arakan |
| | regional civil war | Kayah |
| Burundi | civil war | general |
| | intervention in DR Congo | DR Congo |
| Cambodia | civil war | general |
| Canada | intervention in Afghanistan | Afghanistan |
| Central African Republic | civil war | general |
| Chad | border clashes with Nigeria | border region |
| | civil war | general |
| | intervention in DR Congo | DR Congo |
| Colombia | civil war | general |
| Congo (Brazzaville) | civil war | general |
| | civil war | general |
| Democratic Republic of Congo | civil war | general |
| | transnational war | general |
| Côte d'Ivoire | civil war | general |
| | civil war | general |
| Croatia | war of independence | Slavonia / Krajina |
| | regional civil war | Western Slavonia / Krajina |
| Djibouti | regional civil war | Afar |
| East Timor | war of independence | East Timor |
| Ecuador | interstate border war | border region |
| Egypt | civil war | general |
| El Salvador | civil war | general |
| Eritrea | interstate | border region |
| | war of independence | Eritrea |
| Ethiopia | interstate | border region |
| | against war of independence | Eritrea |
| | civil war | general |
| | externalised civil war | Ogaden border region in Somalia |
| | regional civil war | Oromo region (including across Somali border) |
| | externalised civil war | Mogadishu region of Somalia |
| France | interstate war | Kuwait / Iraq |
| Georgia | civil war | western region |
| | regional civil war | South Ossetia |
| | war of independence | Abkhazia |
| Ghana | regional civil war | northern regions |
| | civil war | Bawku, North-East Ghana |

The table records the status of wars in November 2002.

| War began | Combat status 2002 | Countries |
|---|---|---|
| 1978 | **continuing** | Afghanistan |
| 1997 | suspended by decisive break in action 1997 | Albania |
| 1992 | **continuing** | Algeria |
| 1975 | **suspended by agreement 2002** | Angola |
| 1978 | suspended by decisive break in action 1998 | |
| 1998 | **withdrew 2002** | |
| 1990 | suspended by decisive break in action 1997 (broken agreement 1994) | Armenia |
| 1990 | suspended by decisive break in action 1997 (broken agreement 1994) | Azerbaijan |
| 1973 | suspended by agreement 1997 (previous suspension 1992-96) | Bangladesh |
| 1992 | suspended by agreement 1995 | Bosnia-Herzegovina |
| 1993 | suspended by agreement 1994 | |
| 1948 | suspended by agreement 1994 | Burma |
| 1948 | **continuing** | |
| 1949 | **continuing** | |
| 1991 | suspended by decisive break in action 1992 | |
| 1992 | suspended by decisive break in action 1994 | |
| 1992 | **continuing** | |
| 1988 | **continuing** | Burundi |
| 1999 | withdrew 2001 | |
| 1970 | suspended by decisive break in action 1998 | Cambodia |
| 2001 | **continuing** | Canada |
| 2001 | **continuing** | Central African Republic |
| 1998 | suspended by agreement 1998 | Chad |
| 1965 | **continuing** | |
| 1998 | withdrew in 2000 | |
| 1966 | **continuing** | Colombia |
| 1993 | suspended by agreement 1994 | Congo (Brazzaville) |
| 1997 | suspended by agreement 1999 | |
| 1996 | suspended by decisive break in action 1997 | Democratic Republic of Congo |
| 1997 | continuing despite agreement 2002 and withdrawal of foreign forces | |
| 2000 | suspended by decisive break in action 2001 | Côte d'Ivoire |
| 2002 | **continuing** | |
| 1991 | suspended by agreement 1992 | Croatia |
| 1995 | suspended by agreement 1995 | |
| 1991 | suspended by decisive break in action 1996 | Djibouti |
| 1975 | suspended by agreement 1999 | East Timor |
| 1995 | suspended by agreement 1995 | Ecuador |
| 1992 | suspended by decisive break in action 1998 | Egypt |
| 1979 | suspended by agreement 1991 | El Salvador |
| 1998 | suspended by agreement 2000 | Eritrea |
| 1962 | suspended by agreement 1991 | |
| 1998 | suspended by agreement 2000 | Ethiopia |
| 1962 | suspended by agreement 1991 | |
| 1974 | suspended by agreement 1991 | |
| 1996 | **continuing** | |
| 1996 | **continuing** | |
| 1999 | **continuing** | |
| 1991 | suspended by agreement 1991 | France |
| 1991 | suspended by decisive break in action 1993 | Georgia |
| 1991 | suspended by agreement 1992 | |
| 1992 | continuing 2002 despite agreement 1993 (previous combat 1998) | |
| 1994 | suspended by decisive break in action 1995 | Ghana |
| 1999 | **continuing** | |

# Table of Wars 1990–2002

| Countries | Type of war | Site of war |
|---|---|---|
| Guatemala | civil war | general |
| Guinea | regional civil war | various regions |
| Guinea-Bissau | civil war | general |
| Haiti | civil war | general |
| India | interstate war | Kashmir |
| | regional civil war | Kashmir |
| | regional civil war | Andhra Pradesh, Bihar and Madhya Pradesh |
| | regional civil war | Punjab |
| | regional civil war | Assam |
| | regional civil war | Manipur |
| | regional civil war | Nagaland |
| | regional civil war | Tripura |
| Indonesia | regional civil war | West Papua |
| | war against independence | East Timor |
| | regional civil war | Sumatra/Aceh |
| | regional civil war | Moluccan islands |
| Iran | civil war | general |
| | regional civil war | northwestern Kurdish regions |
| Iraq | regional civil war | northern regions / Kurdistan |
| | interstate war | Iraq / Kuwait |
| | regional civil war | southern Shia regions |
| | interstate clashes: raids by UK and USA | Iraq |
| Israel | civil war | general, including occupied territories |
| Kurdistan | civil war | general |
| Kuwait | interstate war | Kuwait / Iraq |
| Laos | civil war | general |
| Lebanon | general, then regional civil war | southern zone, from 1990 |
| Lesotho | interstate war | general |
| Liberia | civil war | general |
| | civil war | northern regions |
| Libya | civil war | general |
| Macedonia | civil war | North and West |
| Mali | regional civil war | northern Tuareg regions |
| Mauritania | interstate war | border regions |
| Mexico | regional civil war | Chiapas |
| | regional civil war | Guerrero |
| Moldova | regional civil war | Dniestr Republic |
| Morocco | against war of independence | Western Sahara |
| Mozambique | civil war | general |
| Namibia | intervention in DR Congo | DR Congo |
| Nepal | civil war | general |
| Nicaragua | civil war | general |
| Niger | regional civil war | northern Tuareg regions |
| | regional civil war | eastern region |
| Nigeria | border clashes with Chad | border region |
| | regional civil war | northern region |
| Norway | intervention in Afghanistan | Afghanistan |
| Pakistan | interstate war | Kashmir |
| | regional civil war | Karachi / Sind |
| | regional civil war | Punjab |
| Papua New Guinea | regional civil war | Bougainville |
| Peru | civil war | general |
| | interstate war | border region |

The table records the status of wars in November 2002.

| War began | Combat status 2002 | Countries |
|---|---|---|
| 1968 | suspended by agreement 1996 | Guatemala |
| 2000 | **continuing** | Guinea |
| 1998 | suspended by decisive break in action 2000 | Guinea-Bissau |
| 1991 | suspended by decisive break in action 1991 | Haiti |
| 1982 | **continuing** | India |
| 1990 | **continuing** | |
| 1969 | **continuing** | |
| 1981 | suspended by decisive break in action 1993 | |
| 1987 | **continuing** | |
| 1991 | **continuing** | |
| 1978 | suspended by agreement 1997 | |
| 1993 | **continuing** | |
| 1963 | **continuing** | Indonesia |
| 1975 | suspended by agreement 1999 | |
| 1989 | **continuing** | |
| 1999 | **continuing** | |
| 1978 | suspended by decisive break in action 1993 | Iran |
| 1979 | suspended by decisive break in action 1995 | |
| 1974 | suspended by decisive break in action 1997 | Iraq |
| 1990 | suspended by agreement 1991 | |
| 1991 | suspended by decisive break in action 1997 | |
| 1998 | **continuing** | |
| 1948 | **continuing** | Israel |
| 1993 | suspended by decisive break in action 1998 | Kurdistan |
| 1990 | suspended by agreement 1991 | Kuwait |
| 1975 | suspended by decisive break in action 1990 | Laos |
| 1975 | suspended by agreement 2000 clashes since | Lebanon |
| 1998 | suspended by decisive break in action 1998 | Lesotho |
| 1989 | suspended by agreement 1997 | Liberia |
| 1999 | **continuing** | |
| 1995 | suspended by decisive break in action 1997 | Libya |
| 2001 | suspended by agreement 2001 | Macedonia |
| 1990 | suspended by agreement 1995 | Mali |
| 1989 | suspended by agreement 1991 | Mauritania |
| 1994 | suspended by agreement 1995 | Mexico |
| 1996 | ended by decisive break in action 1998 | |
| 1991 | suspended by agreement 1992 | Moldova |
| 1975 | suspended by decisive break in action 1991 | Morocco |
| 1976 | suspended by agreement 1992 | Mozambique |
| 1998 | withdrew 2002 | Namibia |
| 1997 | **continuing** | Nepal |
| 1974 | suspended by agreement 1990 | Nicaragua |
| 1991 | suspended by agreement 1997 | Niger |
| 1994 | suspended by agreement 1997 | |
| 1998 | suspended by agreement 1998 | Nigeria |
| 2000 | **continuing** | |
| 2001 | **continuing** | Norway |
| 1982 | **continuing** | Pakistan |
| 1992 | **continuing** | |
| 1996 | **continuing** | |
| 1988 | suspended by decisive break in action 1997 and by peace agreement 1998 | Papua New Guinea |
| 1980 | suspended by decisive break in action 1999 | Peru |
| 1995 | suspended by agreement 1995 | |

119

# Table of Wars 1990–2002

| Countries | Type of war | Site of war |
|---|---|---|
| Philippines | civil war | general |
|  | regional civil war | Mindanao |
| Russia | regional civil war | North Ossetia / Ingushetia |
|  | civil war | Moscow |
|  | regional civil war | Chechnya |
|  | regional civil war | Chechnya |
|  | regional civil war | Dagestan |
| Rwanda | civil war | general |
|  | intervention in DR Congo | DR Congo |
| Saudi Arabia | interstate war | Kuwait / Iraq |
| Senegal | interstate war | border regions |
|  | regional civil war | Casamance region |
| Sierra Leone | civil war | general |
| Slovenia | war of independence | Slovenia |
| Somalia | civil war | general |
|  | civil war | general |
| Somaliland | civil war | general |
| South Africa | interstate war | Lesotho |
|  | civil war | general |
| Spain | regional civil war | Basque region |
| Sri Lanka | regional civil war | Tamil areas / northeast |
|  | civil war | general |
| Sudan | regional civil war | southern and eastern regions |
|  | regional civil war | Beja |
|  | intervention in DR Congo | DR Congo |
| Suriname | civil war | general |
| Syria | interstate war | Kuwait / Iraq |
| Tajikistan | civil war | general |
| Togo | civil war | general |
| Turkey | regional civil war | south east Kurdish region / northern Iraq |
|  | regional civil war | western region |
| Uganda | regional civil war | northern region |
|  | regional civil war | western region |
|  | regional civil war | central region |
|  | regional civil war | southeastern region |
|  | intervention in DR Congo | DR Congo |
| United Kingdom | interstate clashes | Iraq |
|  | regional civil war | Northern Ireland |
|  | interstate war | Kuwait / Iraq |
|  | intervention in Sierra Leone | Sierra Leone |
|  | intervention in Afghanistan | Afghanistan |
| United States of America | interstate clashes | Iraq |
|  | interstate war | Kuwait / Iraq |
|  | interstate war | Yugoslavia |
|  | intervention in Afghanistan | Afghanistan |
| Uzbekistan | externalised civil war | Kyrgyzstan |
| Venezuela | civil war | general |
| Western Sahara | war of independence | Western Sahara |
| Yemen | civil war | general |
| Yugoslavia | against war of independence | Slovenia |
|  | against war of independence | Croatia |
|  | regional civil war | Kosovo |
|  | interstate war | Yugoslavia |
| Zimbabwe | intervention in DR Congo | DR Congo |

The table records the status of wars in November 2002.

| War began | Combat status 2002 | Countries |
|---|---|---|
| 1969 | **continuing** | Philippines |
| 1974 | **continuing** | |
| 1992 | suspended by decisive break in action 1992 | Russia |
| 1993 | suspended by decisive break in action 1993 | |
| 1994 | suspended by agreement 1996 | |
| 1999 | continuing | |
| 1999 | suspended by decisive break in action 1999 | |
| 1990 | **continuing** | Rwanda |
| 1998 | withdrew 2002 | |
| 1991 | suspended by agreement 1991 | Saudi Arabia |
| 1989 | suspended by agreement 1991 | Senegal |
| 1990 | **suspended by agreement 2002** | |
| 1991 | **suspended by agreement 2002** | Sierra Leone |
| 1991 | suspended by agreement 1991 | Slovenia |
| 1977 | suspended by agreement 1991 | Somalia |
| 1991 | **continuing** | |
| 1991 | suspended by decisive break in action 1995 | Somaliland |
| 1998 | suspended by decisive break in action 1998 | South Africa |
| 1984 | suspended by agreement 1994 | |
| 1968 | suspended by decisive break in action 1992 | Spain |
| | (renewed attacks by ETA starting 2000) | |
| 1977 | **suspended by ceasefire 2002** | Sri Lanka |
| 1983 | suspended by decisive break in action 1990 | |
| 1955 | **continuing despite provisional agreement 2002** | Sudan |
| 1994 | suspended by decisive break in action 1995 | |
| 1998 | withdrew 2001 | |
| 1986 | suspended by agreement 1992 | Suriname |
| 1991 | suspended by agreement 1991 | Syria |
| 1992 | suspended by decisive break in action 1998 | Tajikistan |
| 1991 | suspended by decisive break in action 1991 | Togo |
| 1984 | suspended by decisive break in action 2001 | Turkey |
| 1991 | suspended by decisive break in action 1992 | |
| 1986 | **continuing** | Uganda |
| 1986 | **continuing** | |
| 1994 | suspended by decisive break in action 1995 | |
| 1994 | suspended by decisive break in action 1995 | |
| 1998 | withdrew 2002 | |
| 1998 | **continuing** | United Kingdom |
| 1969 | suspended by agreement 1994 | |
| 1991 | suspended by agreement 1991 | |
| 2000 | withdrew 2001 | |
| 2001 | **continuing** | |
| 1998 | **continuing** | United States of America |
| 1991 | suspended by agreement 1991 | |
| 1999 | suspended by agreement 1999 | |
| 2001 | **continuing** | |
| 1999 | **continuing** | Uzbekistan |
| 1992 | suspended by decisive break in action 1992 | Venezuela |
| 1975 | suspended by decisive break in action 1991 | Western Sahara |
| 1994 | suspended by agreement 1994 | Yemen |
| 1991 | suspended by agreement 1991 | Yugoslavia |
| 1991 | suspended by agreement 1992 | |
| 1998 | suspended by decisive break in action 1999 | |
| 1999 | suspended by agreement 1999 | |
| 1998 | **withdrew 2002** | Zimbabwe |

# REFERENCES

There are four main sources of information of use for tracking the field of war and peace:

- The major reference books, including specialized ones such as *The Military Balance* produced annually by the International Institute for Strategic Studies in London, the *Yearbook* of the Stockholm International Peace Research Institute, or the *Amnesty International* Report, and the more general ones such as *The Statesman's Yearbook* or *Encyclopaedia Britannica.*
- Specialized books, reports and articles, whether academic, activist or more journalistic focusing on a theme or a region of modern conflict or peacemaking. The purely academic studies tend to contribute towards the background against which data choices are made in an exercise such as preparing this atlas, while the activist and journalistic works are rich in the data among which choices have to be made about what to highlight.
- Documents made available by governments, such as the CIA's *World Fact Book*, or the reports, studies and statistics produced by the United Nations on topics from peacekeeping through HIV/AIDS to basic economic conditions.
- The news media.

Much of the material under all four of these headings can be accessed via the internet. Several news media organizations and a large number of research centers and non-governmental organizations now maintain on-line archives that are easily accessible. The reference list below, therefore, includes numerous internet references, some of which offer a number of reports treating problems in depth, some of which offer brisk overviews and chronologies of countries' histories and contemporary conflicts, and some of which (INCORE, for example) are most useful because they systematically organize the information traffic. Many of the internet references have no date on them because they are frequently updated by the organization running that website. Apart from knowing which website(s) to head towards for data on a given issue or country, the best way to get to these and other sources is via www.google.com.

All this means researchers probably visit fewer libraries than before (except virtually) and have to exercise exactly the same care and responsibility in choosing between contradictory information as they have always had to.

*Accord.* London, Conciliation Resources: http://www.c-r.org/accord/index.htm?accser/series.htm
- Clem McCartney, ed. *Striking a balance: the Northern Ireland peace process,* 1999;
- Okello Lucima, ed. *Protracted conflict, elusive peace: Initiatives to end the violence in northern Uganda,* 2002;
- David Lord, ed. *Paying the price: The Sierra Leone peace process,* 2000;
- *Demanding sacrifice: War & Negotiation in Sri Lanka,* 1998;
- *The Mozambican Peace Process in Perspective,* 1998.

Adedeji, Adebayo, ed. *Comprehending and Mastering African Conflicts, The Search for Sustainable Peace and Good Governance.* London and New York: Zed Books, 1999.

Afghan Info Center: www.afghan-info.com

*Afrol:* www.afrol.com

Allison, Graham and J. Grennan (2002). *US Policy on Russian and Caspian Oil exports: Addressing America's Oil Addiction.* Cambridge, Harvard University, John F. Kennedy School of Government.

Amnesty International. *Amnesty International Report* (annual). London, Amnesty International http://www.amnesty.org/ailib/aireport/index.html

ARK: Northern Ireland Social and Political Archive: Conflict Archive on the Internet (CAIN): *The Northern Ireland Conflict (1968 to the Present):* http://cain.ulst.ac.uk

*Ask Asia:* www.askasia.org

*Asia Source:* www.asiasource.org

*Avalon Project at Yale Law School, The: Documents in Law, History and Diplomacy:* http://www.yale.edu/lawweb/avalon/avalon.htm

Baev, Pavel. Russia Refocuses its Policies in the Southern Caucasus. Cambridge Ma: Harvard University, John F. Kennedy School of Government, Caspian Studies Program, Working Paper Series, No. 1, July 2001.

BBC World: Country Profiles & chronologies: http://news.bbc.co.uk/2/shared/bsp/hi/country_profiles/html/default.stm

Brogan, Patric. (1998). *World Conflicts.* Boston Way Lanham, Maryland, Scarecrow Press, Inc.

B'tselem – the Israeli Information Center for Human Rights in the Occupied Territories:
- Yehezkel Lein, *Not Even a Drop: The Water Crisis in Palestinian Villages Without a Water Network*, July 2001: http://www.betselem.org/Download/Not_Even_A_Drop-2001.doc
- Yael Stein, *Israel's Policy of House Demolitions and Destruction of Agricultural Land in the Gaza Strip*, February 2002: http://www.betselem.org/
- Yehezkel Lein, *Land Grab: Israel's Settlement policy in the West Bank*, May 2002: http://www.betselem.org/Download/Land_Grab_Eng.doc

Burg, Stephen L. and P. S. Shoup. *The War in Bosnia Herzegovina, Ethnic Conflict and International Intervention.* New York: M.E. Sharpe, 2000.

Burma Campaign. *About Burma.* http://www.burmacampaign.org.uk/aboutburma.html

Care International, Christian Aid, International Rescue Committee, Oxfam, Save the Children & Tearfund. *The Key to Peace: Unlocking the Human Potential for Sudan.* Interagency report, May 2002, jointly published: http://www.christian-aid.org.uk/indepth/0207sud/keytopeace.pdf

Coalition to Stop the use of Child Soldiers. *The Child Soldiers Global Report 2001:* www.child-soldiers.org

Conetta, Carl. (2002). *The Pentagon's New Budget, New Strategy, and New War.* Cambridge, Ma: Project on Defence Alternatives, 2002 www.co.org/pda/0206newwar.html

Copson, Raymond W. (1994). *Africa's Wars and Prospects for Peace.* New York, M.E. Sharpe, Inc.

Darweish, Marwan and A. Rigby. *Palestinians in Israel: Nationality and Citizenship.* Bradford: University of Bradford, 1995.

*Economist, The*: www.economist.com

*Encarta* homepage www.encarta.msn.com

*Encyclopedia Britannica* http://search.eb.com

Eriksson, John. *The International Response to Conflict and Genocide: Lessons from the Rwanda Experience: Synthesis Report.* Copenhagen, Danish MFA, 1997: http://www.um.dk/danida/evalueringsrapporter/1997_rwanda/

*EurasiaNet Weekly Update* http://lists.partners-intl.net/pipermail/neww-rights/2000-August/000227.html

*Europa World Yearbook 2001.* London, Europa Publications. 2001.

Federation of American Scientists: on-line documents on Ballistic Missile Defense: http://www.fas.org/ssp/bmd/index.html

*Financial Times* www.ft.com.

Glenny, Misha. (2000). *The Balkans 1804-1999, Nationalism, War and the Great Powers.* London, Granta Books.

Global IDP Project. *Database and Profile of Internal Displacement: Sudan (2002).* Oslo: Norwegian Refugee Council and Global IDP Project, 2002: http://www.db.idpproject.org/Sites/idpSurvey.nsf/wCountries/Sudan

Graduate Institute of International Studies, Geneva. *Small Arms Survey 2001.* New York & Oxford, Oxford University Press, 2001.

Griffin, Michael. (2001). Reaping the Whirlwind, The Taliban Movement in Afghanistan. London and Sterling, Virginia, Pluto Press.

*Guardian, The:* www.guardian.co.uk

Gunaratna, Rohan. (2002). Inside Al-Qaeda, Global Network of Terror. London, Hurst and Company.

Human Rights Watch: www.hrw.org
- *World Report 2002*: *http://www.hrw.org/wr2k2/*
- *Slavery and Slave Redemption in the Sudan*, 2002: http://www.hrw.org/backgrounder/africa/sudanupd

ate.htm
- *Afghanistan: Return of the Warlords*, 2002: http://hrw.org/backgrounder/asia/afghanistan/warlords.htm
- *Indonesia: Accountability for Human Rights Violations in Aceh*, 2002: http://hrw.org/reports/2002/aceh/index.htm#TopOf Page

Ichkeria. *The Languages of the Caucasus* http://www.ichkeria.org/english/maps

*Independent, The*: www.independent.cok.uk

International Institute for Strategic Studies, London:
- *The Military Balance 2001-2002*. New York & Oxford: Oxford University Press, 2001.
- *Strategic Survey 2001-2002*. New York & Oxford: Oxford University Press, 2002.

Incore Conflict Data Service Internet Country Guides: http://www.incore.ulst.ac.uk/cds/countries/

Institute for War and Peace Reporting: www.iwpr.net
- *Balkan Crisis Report*
- *Caucasus Reporting Service*
- *Afghan Recovery Report*
- *Reporting Central Asia*
- *Tribunal Update*

International Campaign to Ban Landmines. *Landmine Monitor Report* (annual since 1999). (No place of publication listed) International Campaign to Ban Landmines: http://www.icbl.org/lm/2002/

International Committee of the Red Cross (ICRC): documents and briefings on international humanitarian law: http://www.icrc.org/Web/eng/siteeng0.nsf/iwpList2/Humanitarian_law

International Crisis Group reports: www.crisisweb.org
- *The Loya Jirga: One Small Step Forward?* May 2002;
- *Kashmir: Confrontation and Miscalculation*, July 2002; *Myanmar: The Politics of Humanitarian Aid*, April 2002;
- *Myanmar: The Military Regime's View of the World*, December 2001;
- *Burma/Myanmar: How Strong is the Military Regime?* December 2001;

- *Central Asia: Water and Conflict*, May 2002;
- *Central Asia: Border Disputes and Conflict Potential*, April 2002;
- *Burundi After Six Months Of Transition: Continuing The War Or Winning Peace?* May 2002;
- *Rwanda/Uganda: A Dangerous War of Nerves*, December 2001;
- *Colombia's Elusive Quest for Peace*, March 2002;
- *The Civil Concord: A Peace Initiative Wasted*, (Original version in French) Brussels: Africa Report No. 31, July 201.

*International Herald Tribune* www.iht.com

Judah, Tim. *Kosovo, War and Revenge*. New Haven and London, Yale University Press, 2000.

Kepel, Gilles. *Jihad: The Trial of Political Islam*. London, I.B. Tauris, 2001.

Lewis, Bernard. *What Went Wrong? The Clash Between Islam and Modernity In the Middle East*. London: Weidenfeld & Nicolson, 2002.

Lumpe, Lora., ed. *Running Guns*. London, Zed Books, 2000.

Malcolm, Noel. *Bosnia: a Short History*. London: Macmillan papermac, 1996

Malcolm, Noel. *Kosovo: a Short History*. London: Macmillan, 1998.

Malley Robert and H. Agha. "Camp David: The Tragedy of Errors." *The New York Review of Books*, August 9, 2001.

McDowall, David. *A Modern History of the Kurds*. London, I.B. Tauris, 1997

National Defence Council Foundation. *World Conflict List 2000*: http://www.ndcf.org/Conflict_List/Conflict_Count_2000.htm

*New York Times, The*. www.nytimes.com

Nobel Institute Conflict Map www.nobel.se/peace/educational/conflictmap/conflictmap.html

Norwegian Initiative on Small Arms Transfers: www.nisat.org

Palestinian Academic Society for the Study of International Affairs (PASSIA). *Palestine Facts & Info*: http://www.passia.org/index_pfacts.htm

Peace Now. *34 New Settlement Sites since '01 Elections*, March 2002: www.peacenow.org.il

Rashid, Ahmed. *Taliban, The Story of the Afghan Warlords.* London: Pan Books, 2001.

RightsMaps.com. *Oil and Human Rights in Central and Southern Sudan*
http://www.rightsmaps.com/html/sudmap3.html

Ruthven, Malise. *A Fury for God.* London & New York: Granta Books, 2002.

Salvesen, Hilde. *Guatemala: Five Years After the Peace Accords - The Challenges of Implementing Peace.* Oslo: International Peace Research Institute, 2002:
http://www.prio.no/publications

Shkolnikov, Vladimir. *Recommendations for Democratization Assistance in the Caspian Region.* Cambridge, Harvard University, John F. Kennedy School of Government, 2002.

Shlaim, Avi. *The Iron Wall, Israel and the Arab World.* London: Penguin Books, 2001.

South Asia Analysis Group: www.saag.org

South Asia Intelligence Service: www.satp.org

Stockholm International Peace Research Institute. *Armaments, Disarmaments and International Security. SIPRI Yearbook* (annual). New York & Oxford: Oxford University Press.

*The International Community, the Sudanese Civil War, the Sudan People's Liberation Army, and the future of Sudan.* London: The Sudan Foundation, 1999:http://www.sufo.demon.co.uk/pax015.htm

Transnational Institute. *Merging war: Afghanistan, Drugs and Terrorism. Drugs & Conflict Debate Paper No. 3.* Amsterdam: Transnational Institute, November 2001:
http://www.tni.org/drugs/ungass/index.htm

Turner, Barry. ed. *The Statesman's Yearbook 2001.* London, Macmillan, 2001.

United Kingdom Ministry of Defence. *Operation Fingal Force Composition.* London: Ministry of Defence, December 2001:
http://www.operations.mod.uk/fingal/orbat.htm

United Nations:
• *The Blue Helmets, A Review of United Nations Peace-keeping*, New York: United Nations Department of Public Information, 1996;
• *Report of the Panel on United Nations Peace Operations, (The Brahimi Report).* New York, United Nations, 2000.

www.un.org/peace/reports/peace-operations
• United Nations Integrated Regional Information Network: www.irinnews.org
• Peacekeeping Operations
http://www.un.org/Depts/dpko/dpko/ops.htm

UNAIDS (2002). *The Report on the Global HIV/AIDS Epidemic* ("The Barcelona Report"), XIV International Conference on AIDS, Barcelona, 7-12 July 2002. www.unaids.org

United Nations Development Program:
• *Human Development Report* (annual). New York & Oxford: Oxford University Press:
http://www.undp.org/rbas/ahdr/bychapter.html
• *Arab Human Development Report 2002*:
http://www.undp.org/rbas/ahdr/bychapter.html

United Nations Office on Drug Control and Crime Prevention, *Global Illicit Drug Trends 2002*,
http://www.odccp.org/odccp/global_illicit_drug_trends.html, 2002

United States Central Intelligence Agency, *The World Fact Book.* Washington, DC: CIA Office of Public Affairs, 2002
http://www.cia.gov/cia/publications/factbook/index.html

United States Department of State, Office of the Legal Adviser, Treaty Affairs. *Treaties in Force, 1 January 2000.*
http://www.state.gov/www/global/legal_affairs/tifindex.html

U.S. Committee for Refugees. *World Refugee Surveys: 1999, 2000 & 2001.* USA, Immigration and Refugee services of America 1999.

Vickers, Miranda. *Between Serb and Albanian.* New York: Columbia University Press, 2001.

*Washington Post:* www.washingtonpost.com.

Wood, Brian and Johan Peleman. *The Arms Fixers.* Oslo: International Peace Research Institute, 1999.

World Bank. *World Development Report* (annual), New York & Oxford: Oxford University Press.

# INDEX

Names and countries in timelines,
maps and graphics are not included.